THE REVELATION OF HOPE

A Commentary on
the Book of Revelation

THE REVELATION OF HOPE

A Commentary on
the Book of Revelation

Rob Covell

The Revelation of Hope
A Commentary on the Book of Revelation
Rob Covell

First Edition - June 2019

ISBN #13: 978-1-7325276-3-8
ISBN-10: 1-7325276-3-6

Quest Theological Institute

A Division of Quiver Full Publishing

Cover and inside design layout
Carolyn Covell

Printed in the USA

DEDICATION

I dedicate this book to the amazing Refuge Community family of whom I have had the honor to lead. You are all powerful, brave world-changers who are God's torch bearers for the victorious eschatology that encourages God's people to bear fruit, so that the Lamb who was slain would receive the reward of His suffering.

I also dedicate this work to all who seek the truth, especially in the study of Eschatology, and are brave enough to abandon futurism to see the Revelation as it was received by the First Century Church.

ACKNOWLEDGMENTS

• I first want to acknowledge my beautiful wife, Carolyn, who has loved me through every season of our lives together, and has helped me with the layout and graphic design of this book. I consider her a partner in this work, and I appreciate her many hours of hard work on this project.

• I want to acknowledge, Pastor Dave Collins, my spiritual father, for encouraging me and fighting for my destiny. He is a true apostle of Christ and faithful servant of God. Pastor Dave Collins introduced me to Dr. Harold Eberle's and Martin Trench's book, *Victorious Eschatology*. I am grateful to him for introducing me to a life-changing and faith-building narrative of Covenant Theology and Postmillennialism.

• I want to acknowledge Dr. Kenneth Gentry for his friendship, helping me with this work, visiting The Refuge Community, and writing his wonderful books on Postmillennialism.

• I want to acknowledge Dr. Harold Eberle for spiritually pouring into our church, writing *Victorious Eschatology*, and for his friendship.

• I want to acknowledge Johnny and Elizabeth Enlow for teaching me the practical strategies of loving society through the 7 Mountain Mandate books and conferences. They have introduced me to an exciting and whole new world of societal transformation through the goodness of God. You are great friends, and partners in the Kingdom!

· Lastly, I want to acknowledge the following men and women, though I have not met you personally, your works greatly influenced my spiritual formation in the study of the eschaton: Dr. Jonathan Welton, Dr. Gregg Strawbridge, Cindy Jacobs, and Dr. Gary North.

Thank you!

FOREWARD

Before you begin reading *The Revelation of Hope*, I encourage you to approach this commentary with an open mind, yielded to the Holy Spirit, and considering the view presented in this work is historical, confirmed in world history, and true to the orthodox beliefs of the Christian faith. My goal in writing this commentary is to present to the Body of Christ a victorious, encouraging, and Scriptural work which will empower the Body of Christ to get back to the basics of transforming culture and expanding the knowledge of God in the world through the gospel of Jesus Christ.

In continuing this encouragement to you, the reader, I know what you believe to be true about the end-times (or eschatology) may either be challenged or confirmed. However, as you explore this commentary, you will walk away with an excellent companion to the Book of Revelation that will give you the real history surrounding this amazing prophecy of the Revelation of Jesus Christ and encourage you in your own personal relationship with our King.

QUAERITE, ET SCITIS! (Seek and know!)

CONTENTS

Introduction 15
Chapter One 18
Chapter Two 28
Chapter Three 48
Chapter Four 66
Chapter Five 73
Chapter Six 84
Chapter Seven 94
Chapter Eight 102
Chapter Nine 112
Chapter Ten 124
Chapter Eleven 129
Chapter Twelve 139
Chapter Thirteen 148
Chapter Fourteen 159
Chapter Fifteen 169
Chapter Sixteen 176
Chapter Seventeen 192
Chapter Eighteen 204
Chapter Nineteen 214
Chapter Twenty 229
Chapter Twenty-One 243
Chapter Twenty-Two 254
Resources 261

INTRODUCTION

We all approach the book of Revelation with a narrative that colors how we interpret this prophetic book. Many in the American brand of Christianity approach the book of Revelation with an American-Centric narrative that projects this book into our modern times and colors how we see the future of our country, our world and the future of the church. However, this approach discounts the context of the book, the culture in which it was written and the people it was delivered to. The Futurist view also discounts the real history that confirmed the Book of Revelation to the First Century Church as being from God. In theological terms, we are describing what is called a *hermeneutic*. A hermeneutic is basically the method and preexisting paradigm with which we interpret Scripture.

I mention this because what we believe about the future of the Church (our future) flavors the spirit of our ministries, how we minister, and the message we project to the hearers of our message. If we have a pessimistic or negative view of the future of the Church, the Second Coming of Christ, and the End of the Age, our ministries will reflect that view. The way we pray will be colored with that mindset, and the Gospel we preach will be reflected in that as well. If we have a very positive view of the future return of Jesus Christ, the future of the Church, and the End of the Age, our ministries will reflect that theological construct.

I propose the Futurist approach to Revelation has an expectation of a very bad future for the world, as it predicts all kinds of cataclysmic events and tribulations in the future. We can see this paradigm in the countless movies, books, etc produced by Futurist preachers.

In this study of the Book of Revelation, I am proposing an interpretation of the book that is founded on the context of the culture, the history of the Jews/Romans, and most importantly, the Scriptures. The view I am presenting is a hybrid of the Post-Millennial/Partial Preterist view which I am calling a *Victorious View* of the future. The theological view of the interpretation of Revelation presented in this series emerged very early in Church history, and is supported by many respected theologians, and scholars.

Many people would be shocked to know the Futurist interpretation of Revelation is a little over 150 years old and was founded based upon a trance/vision from a 20-year-old woman named Margaret MacDonald in 1830. It was then propagated by John Nelson Darby and CI Scofield. Futurism is the newest interpretation of the Book of Revelation. We also need to mention an early proto-futurist named Francisco Ribera, a Jesuit Catholic Priest who lived in the late 1500's. He developed his futurism to deflect the assault of the Reformers who claimed that the Antichrist would be a Catholic Pope. Both were wrong. This very pessimistic futurist view of Revelation has affected so many in the church by stealing their hope for the future, the glory and mission of the Church, and has kept us from building a generational expression of Christianity that has its hope founded in the truth of being an overcomer.

Now, let's look at the context of the Book of Revelation, as this is the best way to understand any book of the Bible. When we look at the context and culture to which the book was written to, we build a hermeneutic that is rooted in the real time history of the author and the hearer.

Author: John the Beloved

Date: AD 65-69 – It is important to note that those who hold a futurist view of the book of Revelation must claim a later date for this book, because most of it would have already been fulfilled. There is a mountain of evidence placing the writing of this book during the reign of Nero. The Early Church Fathers also mention John was present in Ephesus in AD 95, being old and infirm, needing to be carried to worship gatherings. There is division regarding the date of this book because the position of Futurists completely falls apart by accepting an early date. *(See* Before Jerusalem Fell, *Dr. Kenneth Gentry for an excellent scholarly approach to the dating of Revelation.)*

Place: Island of Patmos – John mentions the place of these prophetic visions were on the island of Patmos in Revelation 1:9.

Context: This book was written to seven historical churches in Asia Minor, who were shortly going to be facing a horrible wave of persecution and tribulation at the hands of the Jews and the Romans. At this time, the Christian message was a challenge to Jews because it claimed the Church, the Body of Christ, had replaced the Temple as the dwelling place of God; that Jesus Christ ended the Temple sacrifices; and that Old Covenant Judaism was a rejected form of worship by Yahweh. The Christian message was offensive to Rome because Christianity preached no other Lord than Jesus and refused to worship the Caesars of Rome. John's visions were a message from Jesus Himself to strengthen, warn, and encourage the churches to stay true to the Gospel of the Kingdom. Imagine being a First Century Christian and hearing this prophesy for the first time! That is the truest context of this prophecy. Lastly, Revelation 1:3 says "that the time is near", so in that context this was a very relevant letter to them. We owe the Early Church the acknowledgment of overcoming the persecution of Rome, and birthing centuries of the peaceful expansion of our faith.

Type and Shadow: The key to the interpretation of the Book of Revelation is to understand Biblical word pictures and references. We will be focusing on the explanation of these word pictures and present the plain interpretation of these types and shadows throughout our study of the Book of Revelation.

CHAPTER ONE

As we study the Book of Revelation, we will be unlocking the book and demystifying it by understanding its symbolism. So much of the prophetic symbolism is spiritual hyperbole which communicates truth that was common to the culture it was written to. In this first chapter, we will see Jesus described in beautiful prophetic poetry which encourages our spiritual hunger to worship Him and imagine Him in all His Resurrection Glory. We will be comforted to know that no matter what season we are in, He is the faithful Victor who is Lord over everything.

Revelation 1:1-3

a) Revelation – Greek APOKALYPSIS – laying bare, naked, a disclosure of truth, instruction, concerning things that were unknown.

b) Jesus is the Originator of the prophecies of this book. This is not a revelation of the devil, but of the glorious Son of Man.

c) The book is written to the bond-servants of Him, the DOULOS – slave or servile people who regard Him as King.

d) That which will soon take place – EN GINOMAI – Greek – to come into existence soon. This book is naturally to be understood in this context, as being most relevant to the people receiving the book.

e) John writes that the things he saw were faithfully communicated to the churches receiving the Revelation.

f) Blessed – The people who are hearing the prophecy are blessed – Greek – MAKARIOS – Blessed/Happy – to be under the influence of divine favor *(See BARAK in Hebrew)*

g) Time is near – Greek – KAIROS EGGYS – A fixed time when things are brought to crisis, being imminent. We can see from the Greek text this Revelation was expected to be fulfilled quickly - in a short amount of time. We need to be intellectually honest to not impute a long epoch of time in the fulfillment of these prophecies.

Revelation 1:4-5

a) These Seven Churches were real churches located in a specific geographic location at this time. These churches do not represent seven epochs of Church History, and we are not in the Laodicean time of Church History.

b) We see a distinct Trinitarian line of thought in verses 4-5, with the Father, the Sevenfold Spirit of God and Jesus as the faithful witness, and Lord of the kings of the earth. Hebrews 3:1-3 describes Jesus as the true and faithful witness of the Gospel by His death and resurrection.

c) The Sevenfold Spirit or Seven Spirits of God – This is symbolic language for the perfection of the Holy Spirit. The number 7 is the number of perfection or of being complete. What we have here is the typical type and shadow used as the description of the Holy Spirit. This type of allegory or symbolism is used throughout the Revelation. *(See Isaiah 11:1-3)*

d) Verse 5 declares Jesus' love for each of us individually by the pouring out of His blood for each of us on the cross. He freed us! The words in the Greek means to "loose a person or thing from being tied or fastened."

e) These verses serve as an encouragement to the readers of this Revelation who would soon face a season of persecution for their witness as believers in Jesus Christ.

Revelation 1:6

a) We are given the honorable position of being a kingdom for Jesus. This means Jesus rules, has authority over, and leads us as a kingdom. We are His realm of influence as the spiritual Body of Christ in the world.

b) Priests to serve the Father – What a wonderful picture of each of us as representatives of God. Priests offer sacrifices, reveal the knowledge of God, and minister to others. We offer the sacrifices of praise and prayer, we reveal the knowledge of God by our lives, and minister the heart of Father as we heal, prophesy, and demonstrate the power of the Kingdom of God. Priests are also anointed. We are anointed by the Holy Spirit and qualified by Him. The church is the reality and the realization of the type and shadow of the Levitical Priesthood with Jesus as High Priest. The book of Hebrews explains this reality in detail.

Revelation 1:7

a) Verse 7 introduces us to the first interpretation of a prophetic word picture. We need to refer to Matthew 24:30 as we seek to understand verse 7:

Matthew 24:30

1. Sign of the Son of Man in the sky – Josephus documented seven signs in detail. The parallel passage here is Luke 21:11 - "Fearful sights and great signs from heaven."

2. A meteor in the shape of a sword hung over Jerusalem for 12 months of which he eye-witnessed.

3. On the eighth month of Zanthicus before the feast of unleavened bread, a light shone around the altar as bright as the light of day for about ½ hour.

4. At Passover, before the destruction of Jerusalem, a heifer gave birth to a lamb on its way to sacrificial altar. Josephus documents this in detail. This is the same season in which our Lord became the one sacrifice.

5. In the night, a bronze gate to the Temple which required 20 men to close was blown wide open.

6. After a Passover feast, before the setting of the sun, chariots and armed men were seen in the air passing around Jerusalem.

7. At Pentecost that same year, the priests serving in the Temple heard murmuring which eventually became loud voices that said, "Let us depart from here."

8. Josephus says the most fearful sign was a prophet from the lower class, Ananus, during the feast of tabernacles before the destruction of Jerusalem, declared all through the city, "A voice from the east, a voice from the west, a voice from the four winds, a voice against Jerusalem, a voice against bridegrooms and brides, a voice against the whole people." This man was scourged, but showed no sign of fear or pain, he prophesied this over and over,

and became a casualty in the siege from a Roman war engine, as he prophesied his own death.

9. Tribes of the land – not the Earth – Greek word is GE – not KOSMOS or OIKOUMENE. The tribes of the land were the tribes of Israel, not the globe.

10. Again the reference to Jesus coming on the clouds is reference to Him coming in Judgment against the nation and the religious system.

b) Zechariah 12:10 uses the same language found in Matthew 24 & Revelation 1. The thought here is that those who rejected Christ would know the agony of their offense of rejecting Jesus as Messiah and mourn their decision.

c) "Coming on the clouds" is a common Biblical metaphor for the judgment of God. See the following Scripture references. Psalm 18:11-12, Psalm 77:17, Psalm 104:3, Psalm 148:8, Jeremiah 4:13, Ezekiel 30:3, Joel 2:2. The word picture here of Jesus "coming on the clouds" is a reference to His judgment on Jerusalem.

d) The (tribes) peoples of the (earth) land – We need to understand this in context of the Greek. PHYLE – Tribes – those descended from Jacob – GE – Arable land – This is a direct reference to the tribes of Israel, and not a global (KOSMOS) event. The correct understanding of verse 7 is that Jesus is coming to judge the land of Israel, specifically the Temple.

Revelation 1:8

a) Jesus is the beginning and the end and uses the language of everlasting life to declare His Divinity in verse 8. This verse teaches us Jesus is the God-Man.

Revelation 1:9

a) Brother and Companion – ADELPHOS - SYGKOINONOS – Greek word – This means John was "one united to one another by the bond of affection and participant or joint partner."

b) Tribulation or suffering in some translations. The Greek word is THLIPSIS, which means *the pressing*. John was familiar with suffering for the Church of Jesus Christ. His brother James was martyred by Herod Agrippa I around AD 44. Peter and Paul were put to death during the reign of Nero. Both Paul and John were writing to the Church during the reign of Nero, who was a horrible individual, mercilessly persecuting and murdering the faithful. John passed away in Ephesus in AD 98 and was buried there during the reign of Trajan.

c) Kingdom – John identified himself with the being under the authority of a greater King than the one persecuting him. Beloved, which Kingdom are we identifying with?

d) Perseverance proves faith and trumpets our heart! The Church was very young at this point in church history. The Apostles labored as Fathers who longed to see the Church mature to the point of steadfastness, endurance and perseverance.

e) The reason for the pressing was the testimony of Jesus Christ and the Word of God. Reference John 15:18-20 and Luke 6:46-49 – All who claim to have experiential knowledge of Jesus are expected to be faithful to our Bridegroom. Experiencing Jesus builds the grace to endure and overcome all things.

Revelation 1:10-11

a) The Lord's Day – The Early Church set aside the first day of the week for worship, rest and fellowship to observe the resurrection of Jesus Christ. This observance still stands today several millennia later.

b) In the Spirit – What an amazing way to describe the atmosphere of intimately worshiping Jesus. Being "in the Spirit" is the doorway for encountering God. We should have an expectation for encounters as we worship Jesus. We should also consider that in this instance, John being "in the Spirit" is a grace given to him by the Holy Spirit for the express purpose of writing Scripture.

c) The Word of God - Jesus Christ's voice is described like a loud trumpet. The word in the Greek is MEGAS – a mega-loud voice. This indicates the importance of the message Jesus is about to give John. The Lord can speak in a multitude of ways from the still small voice to extreme loud voice. We should be encouraged that however God speaks to each of us - we, being His children - will always hear when we are in the Spirit.

d) Jesus commissions John to write the words of God on a scroll (BIBLION) – a written document, scroll or small book. The Revelation was written to seven real Churches at that time. This truth is one of the keys to understanding the Book of Revelation as it sets the context of what we are reading. It is important to keep in mind we are approximately 2000 years from the events prophesied in Revelation. As we continue in the book, we will see clearly the persons receiving the Revelation would have plainly understood what was delivered to them.

Revelation 1:12-16

a) Seven golden lamp stands – The menorah in Exodus 25:37 is symbolic of the Church of Jesus Christ - who is the light to the world and the fulfillment of this type and shadow found in the Old Testament. Jesus will interpret this prophetic vision later in verses 19-20.

b) One like the Son of Man – This is a direct reference to Daniel 7:13-14. The prophecy in Daniel is confirmed here in verses 13-16. Jesus Christ is revealed in all His glory.

c) Jesus Christ stands among the lamp stands (churches) in glory and authority.

d) Golden sash around the chest – Symbolic of the chords of majestic glory and love emanating from the bosom of Christ for His Bride the Church.

e) Hair white as wool – This is symbolic of the perfect purity of Jesus. The head being the seat of emotion, thought, and decision; Jesus is perfect in pure thoughts, righteous judgments and is perfect in wisdom.

f) Eyes of blazing fire – Symbolic of Jesus' passion for His Bride. His eyes burn with desire for His Beloved. Jesus is unmoved in His loving devotion to redeem mankind and have intimate relationship with people.

g) Bronze feet – Bronze is a metal resistance to corrosion and is a strong alloy. The bronze is a symbol of Jesus being incorruptible and eternal. It is also a picture of His strength as King of Kings and Lord of Lords. This reveals His power and authority as the resurrected Christ.

h) Voice like rushing waters – The voice of Messiah is creative, authoritative and unstoppable. *(See Hebrews 4:12)*

i) Jesus holds the seven stars who are angels that faithfully fulfill their assignments. They are in the right hand of Jesus. The right hand in Scripture is symbolic strength and victory in warfare. *(See Colossians 2:15)*

j) Hebrews 4:12 – Jesus is the Word of God; His words contain creative power and unstoppable decrees. Jesus has victory in His voice. *(See Colossians 1:16; John 1:3-4)*

k) Face as brilliant as the sun – The thought here is that the face of

God is covered in glory and unapproachable light. This is symbolic of the Omniscience of God, who possesses all revelation, knowledge and wisdom. Jesus is the Light. Paul encountered this Light in Acts 9 and described it in Acts 26:13.

Revelation 1:17

a) John was familiar with beholding Jesus as a God-Man, reclining close to His chest, talking with Jesus, walking with Jesus, and touching Him after His resurrection. John now encounters Jesus in preincarnate glory and majesty as God the Son.

b) John falls at His feet as though dead – This glorious display of Jesus overwhelmed the ability of the physical body to stand in His presence. Our physical manifestations are reactions to His presence.

c) Jesus indicates that John was in fear. Perfect love casts out all fear and leaves awe in its place. Jesus tells John do not be afraid and touches Him. A touch from Jesus comforts us, drives out fear, leaving us in awe of Him and ready to do His will.

d) Jesus the First and Last – This description illustrates the truth that Jesus has preeminence in all things. No matter what has touched our lives, Jesus completely sympathizes and understands humanity and has authority over it. *(See Hebrews 7:25)*

Revelation 1:18

a) Jesus conquered the grave. His resurrection proved His victory over death. (Ephesians 4:8) Death is the fruit of the curse from Adam, and Jesus being the Second Adam destroyed the curse of death and gives life. 1 Corinthians 15:45 – Resurrection is one of the great hopes of Christianity, because at the resurrection Eden is restored in fullness. Jesus is eternal life.

Revelation 1:19-20

a) John was commissioned to write about what is now. This

references things which are currently present. This is key to understanding the majority of this prophecy. John was told to write about the current affairs of the time. Greek EIMI – to be present.

b) And what will take place later – Jesus is informing His church regarding their current season and the one to come after it. Jesus is faithful to His Bride and communicates His heart. The Revelation would have been a very comforting book to the First Century Church. They were young, persecuted, engaged in warfare for the faith and needed the blessed comfort of their Risen King.

c) MYSTERION – Greek – that which is hidden – God uses word pictures many times in the Scriptures to communicate deep spiritual truth on a plane that we can understand. The stars are the angels who carry His Word and decrees. We see in Scripture that angels have assignments and messages. This book illustrates the diversity of the spiritual order. Some commentators have suggested the seven stars are people. In this instance, it is my opinion that they are spirits and not men, due to the focus and attention of the spiritual order that is thematic throughout Revelation. The lamp stands are the churches. It would have been comforting to these Seven Churches to know Jesus was with them, walking among them in the spiritual realm.

CHAPTER TWO

Revelation Chapter Two begins the Letters to Seven Churches from Jesus. Each of these seven churches were real churches in real cities. The exhortations to each of them were specific and meaningful to them in the context of their culture and times. These are not seven epochs or seven symbols of the church age. To impute this symbolism to the text is to hyper spiritualize the text. Revelation is a symbolic book, but we should be careful to follow the natural interpretation when it is obvious to us.

In Chapter Two, we will first begin with the Church of Ephesus. This entire chapter introduces us to the encouragements of Jesus Christ for His Bride to overcome, to persevere, and to change their hearts. We see Jesus as the faithful Bridegroom preparing the Bride to walk in victory over the attacks that they were beginning to face at that time. The Letters to the Seven Churches serve as encouragements to us today, as they contain the promises of God to those who hear them. These promises would have provided the motivation and courage to face the persecution that the churches of Jesus Christ were about to experience at the hands of the Romans and the unbelieving Jews.

As we come to the second church, the Church of Smyrna, we find this letter is filled with encouragement for this church that was about to face a time of limited persecution and suffering for Jesus. We also see in this letter the call for this church to persevere, and the promise of the royal eternal crown of life. Jesus describes the type of perseverance the church in Smyrna had obtained in Luke 8:15 - "But the seed in the good soil, these are the ones who have heard the word in an honest and good heart, and hold it fast, and bear fruit with perseverance."

There is no rebuke for the Smyrna church. They received only the defense, comfort and promise of the Savior. He knows their affliction, and will deliver them from it. Lastly, we see Jesus give them the promise of deliverance in the symbolism of the number 10 found in verse 10.

In the third church letter, we find Jesus affirms the Church of Pergamum, and also warns them to change. When Jesus calls us to repentance He does so with a promise.

The fourth letter, the Letter to the Church of Thyatira, highlights the seriousness of spiritual adultery and compromising our faith in Jesus. The church at Thyatira was encouraged in their deeds, love, ministry, perseverance and their growth in these things. However, in the letter to the Church of Thyatira, Jesus corrects them in a way that seems harsh to us, but in the context of the culture of Thyatira, we see a clearer picture of what was needed to be addressed by the Lord so they might have life.

With great correction, comes great promises to the church of Thyatira. They are promised the same authority that Jesus possesses and Jesus promises to give it to those who overcome. The church at Thyatira also gets a double promise of revelation and illumination that come from Jesus.

Throughout the Seven Letters, we see Jesus uses plays on words that would have been meaningful to the people who received the Revelation. My hope is that we begin to see and enjoy the hidden things that are in plain sight in the text, as we continue our study.

Revelation 2:1

a) Ephesus – At this time (AD65-68) Ephesus had an estimated population of 225K. Ephesus was seaport city, with a strong economy, and a it was the seat of government for the Region. The Temple of Artemis was in Ephesus and was considered one of the Seven Wonders of the Ancient World. This church exploded under the ministry of Paul, where the Lord worked extraordinary miracles through Paul. Acts 19 documents the birth of this church. The Ephesian church stormed the mountain of religion and challenged the worship of the false idol Artemis to the point where there was a riot. Christianity was displacing the economy of those who made silver idols.

b) Jesus held the stars in His right hand. The right hand is symbolic of the power and authority of Jesus. The right hand is associated with power in war, strength in battle, and the authority to rule. Jesus is the Lord of Lords, the King of Kings. His messengers or angels carry the authority of His message.

c) Jesus walks among the seven lamp stands. In the last chapter, we looked at the imagery of the seven lamp stands contrasted to the menorah in Exodus 25:37. Jesus is present and walks among His churches, knows their ministries and their hearts as a corporate community of worshipers. He is intimately acquainted with their ways.

Revelation 2:2-3

a) Jesus affirms the Ephesian church, that He knows their deeds. Greek – ERGON – business, employment, the thing which one is occupied by, enterprise or undertaking – This church was occupied in that which God called them to do.

b) Hard work – KOPOS – a beating; beating the breast with grief or sorrow – The Ephesian church knew suffering and persecution. Their success as a church overthrew ungodly powers, and led to a riot in Acts 19. Timothy was martyred at Ephesus as he was evangelizing to a mob who was feasting at the Temple of Artemis. Jesus knows the pain of persecution, the beating of the body and death. Jesus is able to sympathize in fullness with all who endure for Him.

c) Perseverance – Greek – HYPOMONE – Steadfast, constancy, and endurance – Characteristic of a man or woman who is not swayed in their pursuit of faith. This church was unbending in the purity of their doctrine, and faithfulness to Jesus.

d) The Ephesian church walked in a discernment that exposed liars, impostors, and those who claimed to have apostolic authority. Everyone today wants "Apostle" on their business card. It's newest buzz word in Christianity at this season of our faith. While we do not discount that God gives the Body of Christ the gift of the Apostle, we are aware there are many who seek to gain the title, then abuse the title by exerting power through the title. A true Apostle looks like Jesus, and carries the most mature expression of our faith. 2 Corinthians 12:12 – The signs of a true apostle were performed among you with all perseverance, by signs, wonders and miracles.

Revelation 2:4

a) Against you – Greek KATA – to throw down – Jesus has the authority to correct His church. He is being merciful to the church at Ephesus by calling them back to His heart. Hebrews 12:7 – It is for discipline that you endure; God deals with you as with sons, for what son is there whom his father does not discipline? – The Lord carries the authority to discipline children. We need to be very careful when we step into a role of being disciplinarian, as this is a role reserved for the Lord. Keep in mind Jesus is addressing a church, not individuals. As a corporate Body of Christ, we are accountable for the expression of faith in our communities.

b) You have left your first love – Greek – APHIEMI SY PROTOS AGAPE – Divorced or sent away our preeminent Love. The Ephesian church was rich in works, true in doctrine, able to stand up in trials, yet it lacked the passion for its Bridegroom God, Jesus Christ. Jesus is more interested in the exchange of our hearts with Him than in the religious works of keeping a ministry functioning. Paul describes AGAPE love in its fullness in 1 Corinthians 13.

Revelation 2:5

a) Remember the height from which you have fallen – Greek PIPTO to descend to a lower place – This word is verb and speaks of the path which leaves the high place or place of revelation, wonder and worship to descend into a realm devoid of the anointing.

b) Repent – Greek – METANOEO – to change one's mind – Jesus is asking the Ephesian church to remember their early days (Acts 19). Remembering our God story often invokes the passion to love again.

c) When a church (EKKLESIA) no longer functions to seek the heart of the Lord by worshiping Him with passion and love, but rather embraces religious works instead of relationship, her lamp stand is removed. This was never the intent for churches because we have the promise that the gates of hell will not overcome us. We also know the Kingdom we belong to is ever increasing and is everlasting. Our church's destiny depends upon our hearts.

Revelation 2:6

a) To hate the deeds of the Nicolaitans – Greek – MISEO – to hate, to detest – Jesus uses the strongest word for disagreement in this verse. Nicolaitan means *victor over laity* or *destruction of the people.*

b) Jesus loves His Bride. We are His beloved, and He bled for His church! Apparently, there were some in Ephesus who abused their positions of power to rule over the people of God and destroy them. From the very nature of the word Nicolaitan, we assume these leaders sought to rule over God's people. The Lord is the only rightful ruler of His church. His leaders/shepherds are meant to encourage the rule and reign of God in the hearts of His people, not displace Him as King.

Note: Some commentators connect the Nicolaitans with a sect of heretics who taught sexual liberty, drunkenness, and the indulgence of the flesh in light of the grace of God. It is my opinion that this sect is not being mentioned here because they appear about 200 years after this exhortation of Jesus to the Ephesian church was written. I defer to the literal meaning of the text and the implications of the natural definition of the word *Nicolaitan*.

Revelation 2:7

a) Spiritual ears are the ability hear supernatural or spiritual truth and comprehend it. Having the ability to have supernatural or spiritual senses are possible for all Christians because we are indwelt by the Holy Spirit.

b) Jesus offers the Ephesians a promise, not a condemnation.

c) Eating from the tree of life is feasting on the eternal life Jesus gives to His beloved ones. It is not only a promise of heaven in the future but is a reality now through our communing with God. Feeding our spirit by communing with God satisfies our souls, and gives us a first fruits reality of the realms of God.

d) We are overcomers by nature. We can say this with authority because we have the very flame of the Holy Spirit in us. We are in relationship with the Lion of the Tribe of Judah (the tribe of praise). The impartation of His strength in us is our inheritance.

Revelation 2:8

a) Smyrna – root word Myrrh – Located in modern day Turkey, just North of Ephesus, on the Aegean Sea. At this time, Smyrna was a very wealthy and important city during the Hellenistic and Roman eras. Smyrna was a harbor city located on a trade route with an abundance of fresh water from the Meles River. Homer, the famous Greek philosopher, was from Smyrna. One of the most famous marketplaces in the ancient world called the

Agora was located in Smyrna. The Agora is an important key for us later in our study of Revelation 13, when we will be looking at the Mark of the Beast.

b) Smyrna was the seat of Emperor Worship in Asia Minor, and was famous for its round portico buildings on the summit of Mt. Pagos. These buildings were described as "the diadem" as they were considered the crown of culture in that city. Jesus gives John a play on words later in Revelation 2:10 that would have been familiar with the hearers as He offers them the crown of life.

c) The church at Smyrna was probably evangelized by Christians associated with Paul or John, as it was only 35 miles from Ephesus. John was involved with this church as he appointed Polycarp to be its Bishop/Leader.

d) Polycarp, a protégé of John, was from Smyrna. He was Bishop in Smyrna and was martyred at 80 years of age. He would have been present when the Revelation was delivered to the church at Smyrna. Irenaeus said this about Polycarp, "Polycarp also was not only instructed by apostles, and conversed with many who had seen Christ, but was also, by apostles in Asia, appointed Bishop of the Church in Smyrna...always taught the things which he had learned from the apostles, and which the Church has handed down, and which alone are true."

e) Jesus' words have eternal authority, as He is the First and the Last. This means Jesus has preeminence in all things, and possesses eternal life within Himself. Jesus died and was resurrected. Our whole faith system hangs on not only on Jesus' sacrifice for sin, but also His resurrection from the dead. His resurrection is important because it qualifies Him to be able to offer eternal life to us. Jesus is comforting this church with that very truth. They can be assured their faith will deliver them from the persecution they were about to face, and from the death many of them would face as martyrs.

Revelation 2:9

a) Smyrna was a very wealthy city at this time and the wealth of Smyrna revolved around the Agora. The Agora was the place of culture, business, and the trades. The Christian church, being taught Jesus was King of Kings, Lord of Lords and the Savior of all, would have avoided the system of mammon in Smyrna because it revolved around Emperor Worship. The city was wealthy; they were poor (*beggary* in the Greek) because of their fidelity to Christ, however, Jesus tells them they are rich in Him. In Luke 12:21, Jesus tells us we should be rich toward God. The church of Smyrna was rich in God.

b) The slander/blasphemy – Greek – BLASPHEMIA – to slander a good name; speak in an injurious way about someone. The Jews who rejected Jesus as Messiah considered the followers of Christ as heretics. They made claim to be the people of God, to possess His Covenant, and host His presence at the Temple in Jerusalem. The Christian Church, on the other hand, taught *they* had a New Covenant given to them by God, that *they* were the Temple, and that *they* hosted the presence of God *within themselves* by receiving the Holy Spirit. Naturally, the Jews who rejected Jesus as Messiah in Smyrna were speaking against the teaching of the Church. At this time, the Temple and Church coexisted until AD70. Romans 2:29 – But he is a Jew who is one inwardly; and circumcision is that which is of the heart, by the Spirit, not by the letter; and his praise is not from men, but from God.

c) Jesus is affirming the church of Smyrna that they are the people of God. Jesus even calls the Jews who were slandering them a synagogue of Satan. Any place of worship that does not worship Jesus is not partnered with Jesus. We see the Jewish persecution of the Church throughout the book of Acts, and finally ending in AD 70, when the Temple was destroyed.

Revelation 2:10

a) Perfect love casts out fear – This church was encouraged to not fear, as fear would rob them of their glory as the people of God and the integrity of their message. Fear – Greek – PHOBEO – to be put to flight; to be scared away.

b) It is the devil who brings persecution, pain and suffering to people. Jesus came to give life to the full. The assignment of the enemy is in contrast to the comforting words of Jesus to His church in Smyrna. The devil may be the author of the imprisonment of God's people in Smyrna, but faith cannot be imprisoned. *(See Acts 16:16 & Acts 12)*

c) Persecution for ten days – This is symbolic and not literal. Jesus is telling the church that their suffering and persecution is limited and will pass. Ten is the number of God's word and of God's works. We have 10 Commandments, Passover was on the 10th Day of the first month, and The Day of Atonement was on the 10th day of the 7th month. God sent 10 plagues upon Egypt. The church of Smyrna was going to be delivered by the God of the 10's!

d) Jesus offers them a real crown of eternal royalty and victory all in the backdrop of the crowned rich city of Smyrna that boasted a false diadem of wealth and power.

e) Jesus calls them to be faithful – Greek – PISTOS – trusty, faithful, of persons who show themselves faithful in the transaction of business, the execution of commands, or the discharge of official duties

Revelation 2:11

a) We can only receive spiritual revelation and illumination from God when our spirits are open to hearing. God speaks in veiled language which can only be understood in the context of relationship with Him. All Christians are given the grace to hear Him as we claim to have not only a relationship with God, but we also claim to have His very flame in us in the Person of the Holy Spirit.

b) Hearing His word impacts us to the point of unwavering faith, as His word contains authority, power and creativity to form in us all we need.

c) Not being hurt by the second death – This is deliverance from the Great White Throne Judgment – Revelation 20:11-15

d) The Scriptures teach Adam gave us the inheritance of death as mankind's first representative before God. Jesus, who is the Second Adam, gives us life as God's perfect representative born as a Man. Romans 5:14, 1 Corinthians 15:22, 1 Corinthians 15:45 – Jesus will not allow us to be admitted into to eternal judgment which is the second death in the spiritual reality we call hell.

e) Scripture comforts us with these words: 2 Corinthians 5:8 – We are of good courage, I say, and prefer rather to be absent from the body and to be at home with the Lord.

f) There is no call to repent or change course for this church, as they were already moving in the perseverance of faith.

Revelation 2:12

a) Pergamum – Located 16 miles inland from the Aegean Sea, on the North side of the Caicus River. It was founded in ancient times around 400BC, was a center of culture, and a strategic military site due it being positioned on high ground. This was a very important city in terms of learning, medical science, and innovation. The city population at the time of Revelation was approximately 200K.

b) At the time this church letter was written, Pergamum boasted a huge stone throne dedicated to Zeus/Jupiter. It was also a famous healing center of the ancient world. Hippocrates, the famous ancient, was from Pergamum. This is where we derive the Hippocratic Oath doctors take when they finish medical school. Hippocrates is considered the Father of Western Medicine. The medical symbol of the snake around the pole originated from Pergamum. The healing center in Pergamum was called the *Sanctuary of Asclepius*.

c) Pergamum had a library that rivaled the library of Alexandria, Egypt. Parchment was invented at Pergamum.

d) This church was known to the Apostle John, as he had a close relationship with Antipas, whom John appointed leader of the church of Pergamum. This church was evangelized in a similar way as the church of Smyrna was evangelized. Christians from Ephesus would have evangelized this city.

e) Jesus is the One with the sharp double-edged sword. Hebrews 4:12 – For the word of God is living and active and sharper than any two-edged sword; piercing as far as the division of soul and spirit, of both joints and marrow, and able to judge the thoughts and intentions of the heart. The words of Jesus carry the authority to decree Divine Justice, carry creative power, bring correction and wage war against everything that opposes His heart. Jesus is calling the church of Pergamum to the revelation of His power, and the mightiness of His Name. It is important to remember that the Seven Letters are addressed to whole communities, not to individuals. As church communities, we are accountable to our expression of Christianity.

Revelation 2:13

a) Jesus knows the condition of cities and the regional spiritual strongholds that exist within them. In Pergamum, Jesus says Satan has his throne. It is interesting to note that in Pergamum, there was a large stone throne dedicated to Zeus/Jupiter. It was a huge edifice on top of mountain. The city who was boasting to have an altar throne to a false god was actually ruled by the

One on the true throne of heaven, Jesus Christ.

b) True to My Name – Greek – KRATEO – to have power, to be powerful – This church was not simply remaining true, they were standing in power. The church at Pergamum was faithful to their King, Jesus.

c) To renounce – Greek – ARNEOMAI – to deny or to act out of character – The church at Pergamum was faithful to their identity as God's own people.

d) Antipas – appointed by the Apostle John as leader of the church at Pergamum. Antipas was martyred by being burned in a brazen bull-shaped altar used for casting out demons that were worshiped in Pergamum. Antipas was taunted by the crowd, "Antipas, the world is against you!" Antipas answered, "Then I am against the world." This human sacrifice of a believer did not shake the faith of this church. Revelation 6:9 tells us that those who are martyred will be avenged by God.

Revelation 2:14-15

a) There were two factions in the church at Pergamum who were robbing the church of her purity and identity. The teachers of Balaam were robbing the church of purity, and the Nicolaitans were robbing the church of her identity as a royal priesthood and a holy nation.

b) Balaam – Numbers 22-25 – A compromised prophet who was spiritual adulterer and who prophesied for gain. He was an extravagant worshiper, as mentioned in Numbers 22. However, he knew he could not curse Israel, but advised Balak, the King of Moab, to have the women of Moab seduce the men of Israel, so that the Lord would punish them for their immorality and spiritual adultery. Balaam was killed in battle (Joshua 13:22). The thought here is that there were those in the church at Pergamum, who were committing spiritual adultery and using their prophetic gift to satisfy their own desires and will.

c) The Nicolaitans were previously mentioned in the letter to Ephesus. Jesus loves His Bride. We are His beloved, and He bled for His church! There were some in Pergamum who used their positions of power to rule over the people of God and destroy them. From the very nature of the word Nicolaitan *(victor over laity)*, we assume these leaders sought to rule over God's people. The Lord is the only rightful ruler of His church. His leaders/shepherds are meant to encourage the rule and reign of God in the hearts of His people, not displace Him as King.

d) Jesus is bringing correction to a community of Christians who were compromised by those with agendas.

Revelation 2:16

a) Repent – Greek – METANOEO – to change one's mind. Our thoughts carry the ability change course and re-align ourselves with God. This is the power of a transformed mind. A transformed mind is mind that has repented. Romans 12:2 – And do not be conformed to this world, but be transformed by the renewing of your mind, so that you may prove what the will of God is, that which is good and acceptable and perfect. Jesus always offers a promise when He calls us to repentance.

b) The sword of my mouth – It is the word of God that stands as the ultimate authority over churches, and individual lives. Heresies and false teachings are always defeated by the truth contained in the Word of God.

c) It is important to remember the Church of the First Century was very vulnerable. They did not have the canon of the New Testament, but probably one of the Synoptic Gospels, and maybe a few Apostolic letters. It would have been difficult to resist bad doctrine because they lacked the full counsel of the New Testament. They were also existing side by side with

Judaism, preaching they were the extension of God's plan of salvation for the world. They declared the followers of Jesus Christ were God's people. *(See Peter 2:4-9)*

Revelation 2:17

a) To him who overcomes – Hidden manna – Greek – KRYPTO MANNA – Concealed bread – This speaks of feasting on Jesus in the secret or hidden place. Jesus is promising revelation in intimacy. So many things can be implied by the use of these symbolic words. The person who has given themselves to hear Him and seek Him will indeed be satisfied and rewarded by knowing God.

b) White stone – In a Roman Court of Law, one was acquitted by being given a white stone to indicate innocence. When we are in Jesus Christ, we are a new creation with a new name. (2 Corinthians 5:17) Saul became Paul; Simon became Peter; Solomon became Jedidiah. We will be called by an intimate new name by God which we alone share with Him.

Revelation 2:18

a) Thyatira – Located in modern day Turkey, approximately 50 miles inland from the Mediterranean Sea. It was a border town between Lydia and Mysia. The name Thyatira means *Daughter*, and was named by King Seleucas Nicator after he was told his wife had given birth to a daughter (290BC).

b) Thyatira was located on a trade route, and was known as a city of commerce. Thyatira is listed as having the most trade guilds of any ancient city of that time. This information will be very helpful to us in understanding the letter to Thyatira. Thyatira was famous for the dyeing of cloth, especially the color indigo (or purple). Acts 16:13-15 tells us about Lydia who was from Thyatira, and was a dealer for this type of cloth. Paul and Silas probably ministered there as they traveled through that area. The church of Thyatira played no major roles in church history.

c) Jesus describes Himself in a way which parallels Daniel 10:5-6 – I lifted my eyes and looked, and behold, there was a certain man dressed in linen, whose waist was girded with a belt of pure gold of Uphaz. His body also was like beryl, his face had the appearance of lightning, his eyes were like flaming torches, his arms and feet like the gleam of polished bronze, and the sound of his words like the sound of a tumult.

d) Eyes of blazing fire – Symbolic of Jesus' passion for His Bride. His eyes burn with desire for His Beloved. Jesus is unmoved in His loving devotion to redeem mankind and have intimate relationship with people. Jesus is passionate for the church of Thyatira and desires a pure spotless Bride.

e) Bronze feet – Bronze is a metal resistant to corrosion, and is a strong alloy. The bronze is a symbol of Jesus being incorruptible and eternal. It is also a picture of His strength as King of Kings and Lord of Lords. This reveals His power and authority as the resurrected Christ. The church of Thyatira needed encouragement to deal with the false teaching and the compromise in their community.

Revelation 2:19

a) Jesus knows the condition of our church communities. The Thyatiran church had progressed in deeds. The word for deeds in Greek is ERGON – business, employment, that which one is occupied by. Jesus repeats the word twice in verse 19, to affirm their progress in faith works. James 2:18 – Show me your faith without deeds, I will show you my faith by what I do. Faith is an action word that moves toward the object of our faith.

b) The church of Thyatira was progressing in deeds and service because they were growing in love and faith. They were expressing AGAPE and PISTIS. The word for service in the Greek is DIAKONIA – those who by the command of God promote religion among men.

c) This church was persevering in faith and love, meaning they were steadfast and constant in deeds, service, love, and faith.

d) Jesus is going to bring a word of correction to this church, but Jesus always corrects with hope and promise. Keep in mind Jesus is addressing a body of believers and not isolating individuals. Our communities are accountable for our expression of Christianity.

Revelation 2:20

a) Prophetess Jezebel – The problem here is not a woman who is a prophetess in the church of Thyatira. We must remember Revelation is a prophetic book. It is best understood in the context of the culture, the history of God's people at the time, and by allowing Scripture to interpret Scripture. What we are seeing here is the spirit of Jezebel in operation in this church.

b) Jezebel – Introduced to us in 1 Kings 16:31. She was the Sydonian wife of King Ahab who was King of Israel. Her name means *unchaste,* so the mention of her name here in Revelation gives us a clue to the spirit in operation.

c) Jezebel killed the prophets of the Lord and promoted the prophets of Baal. The Jezebel spirit persecutes those who are anointed to carry the Word of the Lord, and it promotes spiritual adultery.

d) Jezebel murdered Naboth for his vineyard land/inheritance in Israel (1 Kings 21). Jezebel used false accusation to murder Naboth by stoning him to death. The Jezebel spirit uses deception to kill the faith of God's people and steal their inheritance in God.

e) Jezebel practiced and promoted spiritual adultery and witchcraft. *(See 2 Kings 9:22)*

f) Jezebel was executed by Jehu, and died as prophesied

by Elijah in 2 Kings 9:36. Jezebel was thrown from a window by eunuchs. This was the most disgraceful death ever recorded in Scripture.

g) Understanding Jezebel as a type and shadow helps us to understand the charges Jesus is bringing to the Thyatiran church. The whole commerce and culture of Thyatira revolved trade guild associations. Trade guilds were dedicated to patron Greek gods and demigods. To belong to a trade guild, one would need to take oaths, offer sacrifices, feast with meat dedicated to idols, and participate in wild partying that accompanied the feasts. A Christian would have been in a very difficult position in terms of employment and finances without compromising their faith.

h) British Bible scholar William Barclay. – "These guilds met frequently, and they met for a common meal. Such a meal was, at least in part, a religious ceremony. It would probably meet in a heathen temple, and it would certainly begin with a libation to the gods, and the meal itself would largely consist of meat offered to idols. The official position of the church meant that a Christian could not attend such a meal."

i) Sexual Immorality – Greek – PORNEUO – to prostitute one's body to the lust of another, to give one's self to unlawful sexual intercourse. Metaphorically – spiritual adultery.

j) We can conclude there were those in the church of Thyatira who were teaching God's people that it was acceptable to compromise their faith in regard to their membership and participation in the trade guilds, thus committing spiritual adultery and participating in idolatry.

Revelation 2:21

a) The Lord is merciful, patient and longsuffering. Numbers 14:18 – The LORD is slow to anger and abundant in lovingkindness, forgiving iniquity and transgression; but He will by no means clear the guilty, visiting the iniquity of the fathers on the children to the third and the fourth generations. Jesus is being merciful in allowing time for repentance. It is the kindness of God that leads us to repentance. *(See Romans 2:4)*

b) Repent – changing the mind which leads to the changing of the direction of a person's life.

c) Repent of her immorality – Greek – PORNEIA – illicit sexual intercourse of all types; metaphorically – of the defilement of idolatry, as incurred by eating the sacrifices offered to idols

d) She was unwilling – Greek – OU – no, not; in direct questions expecting an affirmative answer – The Lord had offered the invitation for a heart change and it was refused.

Revelation 2:22

a) Those who commit adultery with her – It was unlikely there was one prophetess who was sleeping with members of the church. It is more likely there were those who were agreeing with the compromise being offered by the false teachers/prophets in the church of Thyatira.

b) The bed is symbolic of the place of rest and healing. Jesus' relationship with his church was being compromised and corrupted by the false teachers/prophets. The bed here is not a bed that is slept on, but a bed that a sick person is carried on.

c) Jezebel, being cast onto a bed of suffering, describes the effects spiritual adultery and compromise as it is spiritual sickness.

d) Suffer intensely – MEGAS THLIPSIS – Great tribulation, pressing, pressure – metaph. Oppression, affliction, tribulation, distress, straits – When we leave truth, and the protective grace of God, we are open to reaping what we have sown. *(See Galatians 6:7-8)*

e) Repentance always draws us back into the full benefit of grace.

Revelation 2:23

a) I will kill her children with pestilence [NASB] – This is a more accurate translation of verse 23. Jesus is not in the business of death. John 10:10 – The thief comes only to steal and kill and destroy; I came that they may have life, and have it abundantly.

b) Jesus does not give death, however He is Judge. What is in view here is symbolic language describing the spiritual death of the heretic and apostate. Those who corrupt their faith often lead future generations into a corruption that gets farther and farther away from the truth, and thus are dead children in terms of New Covenant life.

c) The True Church/Body of Christ can easily recognize error and judge the fruits of lost religious movements. The Christian church throughout church history was marked by love, power, miracles, healing, dead raising, spiritual gifts, and encounters with God. Anything less is not normative of the Christian experience we see starting in the book of Acts.

d) Jesus searches minds and hearts – The Lord knows the true condition of our hearts, and will minister and guide us according to our need.

e) Christians are benefited by living in mystical union with God. We have been mystically united to Christ, and the realization of our identities in Him opens the grace for us to excel and benefit in faith.

Revelation 2:24-25

a) Deep Secrets – There were those in Thyatira who did not

participate in the spiritual adultery that was being taught in their community. One does not have to strive to know the mysteries of the Kingdom, as we have the Holy Spirit to teach us. It is our inheritance in Jesus Christ to know the mysteries of the Kingdom. Any teaching that does not present us an on-ramp to encountering God and loving Him passionately should be tested. Esoteric teachings do not originate in God because it is His desire for us to know Him and be close to Him. All deep secrets come from Satan. He is darkness – God is light.

Revelation 2:26-27

a) The promise to the one who overcomes is the authority of Psalm 2. Purity of faith always yields maximum authority. We see this principle in Acts 19, with the Sons of Sceva misusing the Name of Jesus, and Paul mentioned having the full authority connected to the Name of Jesus.

b) We have victory written on our hearts. We are overcomers by our new nature given to us by Jesus Christ and imparted by the Holy Spirit.

Revelation 2:28

a) Morning Star – The morning star is the promise of the day to come. Jesus is the promised Light of Dawn which brings the light of revelation and illumination to our hearts. 2 Peter 1:19 – So we have the prophetic word made more sure, to which you do well to pay attention as to a lamp shining in a dark place, until the day dawns and the morning star arises in your hearts.

b) Spiritual ears have the ability hear supernatural or spiritual truth and comprehend it. The ability to have supernatural or spiritual senses are possible for all Christians because we are indwelt by the Holy Spirit.

CHAPTER THREE

Chapter Three continues with the Letters to the Seven Churches. The first letter in Chapter Three is the Letter to the Church of Sardis. This church struggled with being tempted to mingle Judaism and Christianity to the point that the grace and truth that are in Jesus Christ was being blurred. Paul fought this theological battle in Galatians. Hebrews also clearly confronts the temptation to continue to embrace the Old Covenant to the point where the truth of the New Covenant is lost.

There are three very amazing promises offered to those in Sardis who overcome. Jesus does not commend this church, but offers this church glory in return for repentance. It is the grace and the goodness of God to give us beauty for ashes.

The next letter is to the church of Philadelphia. In the Letter to the Church of Philadelphia, Jesus did not give this church any correction, but gave them promises of deliverance from trials, and four eternal spiritual promises that are staggering in scope. The Lord always gives the most lavish gifts and graces to His children.

The following is some background on ancient Philadelphia which will help us see this letter in the context of those who received it:

1. Located in Modern Day Turkey about 50 miles inland on a low sloping hill, in the Hermus Valley, Philadelphia was founded in 189BC by King Eumenes II of Pergamum.

He named the city in honor of his brother who would be his successor, as he had no heir. King Eumenes II was nicknamed "the one who loves his brother" (Philadelphia).

2. This city was very similar in culture to Sardis, as it was located on the same trade route, and was known for being the epicenter of Emperor Worship. The city coins had the inscription NEOKORON – which means "keeper of the temple". The city suffered significant damage by an earthquake in AD17, and was given aid by Tiberius. In return they honored him with a temple. At the time the Revelation was given to the Church of Philadelphia, it was a prosperous wine grape growing region. The cult of Dionysus revolved around the wine industry.

3. A sizable Jewish population lived there in the First Century which persecuted the Church of Philadelphia. Christianity at this time was considered a Jewish Messianic heresy, and was still not entirely distinct or separated from Judaism. It is important to keep in mind that the Temple in Jerusalem was still standing and that the Church and Temple stood side by side for about 40 years, preaching competing messages. The Church was preaching a New Covenant in the Person of Jesus Christ, and the Jewish people who rejected Jesus as Messiah preached the continuance of the Old Covenant. These were polar opposite understandings of the Scriptures, and were the fuel for persecution. We see these persecutions in Acts 19, Acts 4, Acts 7, Acts 8, Acts 13:50, Acts 14:19, Acts

17:5, Acts 18:6, Acts 21:27, Acts 23, Acts 25:7

4. The Church of Philadelphia was prosperous from the First Century to Medieval Times. Many Orthodox Christians still live there today. The city is now called Alaehir.

At the end of Chapter Three, we will conclude the Seven Letters to the Seven Churches with our final look at the Church of Laodicea. The Laodicean church has been the source material for many condemning sermons, exhortations, and warnings to shock the Modern Body of Christ and instill fear in the hearts of the Beloved that Jesus might "spit them out of His mouth!" However, the historical context of the Letter to Laodicea shows that Jesus used a play on words three times when He addressed this community, and these references would have stirred the hearts of believers in Laodicea to repent and change the course of their churches' futures.

It is true that this church receives no praise from their Lord, and is rebuked in a very forceful way, but this church also is promised two of the loveliest and most intimate promises when compared to the promises offered to the other six churches.

The following are some facts about Laodicea that will help understand the context of this letter from Jesus to this Church:

1. The city of Laodicea was founded by Antiochus II, approximately 263BC and named after his wife Laodice. It is located in Modern Day Turkey, and is about 100 miles East of Ephesus, and was located on a major trade route.

2. The city was very prosperous and wealthy due to it being a major trade center of that region. Scholars call it a convergence city because it was meeting point of multiple regions. The wealth of those regions flowed into Laodicea.

3. It was cultural center for the arts, science, medicine, banking and trading in fine goods.

There was a sizable Jewish population in Laodicea, however the church at Laodicea was not persecuted by the Romans or the Jews in Laodicea. This was due to the healthy economy and the ease of life in Laodicea. Where there is an even distribution of prosperity there is usually peace among the citizenry.

4. During Nero's reign, the city was completely destroyed by an earthquake. The city was so prosperous the people who rebuilt it did not take any loans or aid from the Empire.

5. The Church at Laodicea was known by the Apostle Paul and evangelized by Epaphras (Colossians 4:12). It is also credited as being led by a female Pastor named Nymphas (Colossians 4:15). Paul wrote a letter to the Laodiceans and unfortunately it has been lost (Colossians 4:16). Apparently, the Holy Spirit decided it was not worthy to be Canon.

In the end of our study of the Seven Letters to the Seven Churches, I want to remind us that seven is the number of finished or complete works in the Scriptures. These letters do not symbolize Seven Ages of Church History, but they do present us with the whole counsel of God regarding the things Church communities need to be aware of and are warned by.

Revelation 3:1

a) Sardis – Located in Modern Turkey 50 miles inland from the Mediterranean Sea, and in the middle of the Hermus Valley. In ancient times, the region was called Lydia. A King named Croesus made Sardis famous because of the great wealth from the deposits of Electrum (alloy of Gold and Silver). Croesus was the first person to produce standardized coinage in history. Sardis means *red ones*.

b) Cyrus the Persian King – Isaiah 44:28 & 2 Chronicles 36:22 – defeated Croesus. Cyrus freed the Jews in Babylon and aided the effort to rebuild the Temple in Jerusalem. *(See Ezra 5:11-16)*

c) Sardis had a sizable Jewish population which is mentioned by the Historian Josephus in his *Antiquities*. This is important to our study, because the Christian Church and Jewish community in Sardis lived side by side. Sardis had the largest synagogue in the ancient world. Many church historians note the Christian Church was deeply influenced by the Circumcision Movement mentioned in Acts 15 and was addressed directly in Galatians & Hebrews. It struggled with what church historians call Jewish/Christian Syncretism. It is important to understand that at this time, the Christian Church was considered a Jewish heresy. The New Covenant and the Old Covenant (the Temple) co-existed for about 40 years.

d) Melito was a famous theologian and the first leader of the Church in Sardis after the Apostolic Era. It is said that Melito knew the Apostle John, although this cannot be substantiaed. Melito kept many Jewish customs including Passover, Sabbath, and stayed true to the celebration of the resurrection of Jesus Christ according to the Passover Calendar. Melito wrote about this in his famous Paschal Homily. Melito also was a forerunner in the explaining the Hypostatic Union (Jesus is fully Divine and fully Man). Melito probably was not born when the church of Sardis received the Revelation, but would have been the next generation of leaders to succeed those who did.

e) Jesus identifies Himself as the One who holds the Seven Spirits or Sevenfold Spirit – The Sevenfold Spirit or Seven Spirits of God – This is symbolic language for the perfection of the Holy Spirit. Seven the number of perfection or of being complete. What we have here is the typical type and shadow used as a description of the Holy Spirit. This type of allegory or symbolism is used throughout the Revelation. *(See Isaiah 11:1-3)* Scripture teaches us the Holy Spirit comes forth from the Father and Jesus. We see this same reference in Revelation 1:4, Revelation 4:5 & Revelation 5:6.

f) Jesus holds the seven stars – Revelation 1:20 – The seven stars are the seven angels of the churches being addressed in the Letters to the Seven Churches. Whether these are Pastors/ Leaders of these churches, or whether they are spiritual messenger angels is not important. What is important is that Jesus holds His messengers in his hand. It is comforting to know that we are gripped in the loving hands of Jesus, held in the nail scarred hands of salvation, eternally secure. Those who have His Word are held in His hands.

g) I know your deeds – The word for deeds in Greek is ERGON – business, employment, that which one is occupied by. The church of Sardis was busy in works. From the outward appearance they looked alive by their works, but the true condition of the church at Sardis was spiritual death. Greek – NEKRON – one who has breathed his last – devoid of animate life – Metaphor: spiritually dead.

h) Galatians teaches us the Law was good, but it could not bring life. Galatians 2:16 – "Nevertheless knowing that a man is not justified by the works of the Law but through faith in Christ Jesus, even we have believed in Christ Jesus, so that we may be justified by faith in Christ and not by the works of the Law; since by the works of the Law no flesh will be justified."

i) The consensus among church historians is that the church at Sardis was compromising their faith by religious works of the Law, just like the Galatian heresy.

Revelation 3:2

a) Wake up! Greek – GREGOREO – to watch – metaph. – give strict attention to, be cautious, active – to take heed lest through remission and indolence some destructive calamity suddenly overtakes one. Jesus is sounding the trumpet of alarm. This is a loud shout to the Bride. Jesus is faithful and communicates His heart in any way possible for His Bride to hear.

b) Strengthen what remains – Greek –STERIZO – to make stable – to set in place. Deeds that make us complete are belief in the gospel of Jesus Christ. Belief and faith require a response. When Jesus addressed the rich young ruler in Mark 10, He told him to sell all his possessions. Selling the possessions would not save him, but selling them would prove the condition of his heart in regards to having faith in Jesus and accepting Jesus' invitation to follow Him.

c) In the sight of – The motives of our hearts are open books before the gaze of the Father.

Revelation 3:3

a) Remember – Greek – MNEMONEUO- to be mindful of – to think of and feel for a person or thing – Remembering our testimonies, the mercies of God in our lives, and our histories in God are the guardians of our faith. These things increase thanksgiving and gratefulness to the Lord.

b) The church at Sardis received the grace of God in the Person of Jesus Christ, and heard about the great works of His love. G. Davis Dean, in his book, *The Revelation of Jesus Christ*, writes there were some in the Christian community of Sardis who so co-mingled their faith that they were admonished for swearing oaths in the synagogues, and seeking rabbis for healing rituals.

c) Repentance is changing our minds to agree with God, and moving in the direction of His destiny for us. Repentance is not only about overt sin, but can also pertain to the choices we make every day that lead us either into destiny or out of destiny.

d) Jesus coming like a thief – Many of us have been lead to believe this is speaking about His return. Jesus Christ certainly does return. However, this is a play on words. Alfred Edersheim quotes the Talmud, "Those who were sleeping on the Temple watch and were caught doing so were beat and had their garments burned. The Captain of the Guard was the "thief in the night" who came in the night watches to verify that all was secure." Jesus is giving a warning not be caught off guard, and sleeping in regards to the truth of gospel. This was common idiom in Jewish Culture, and the church of Sardis, having deeper Jewish roots than the other churches in Asia Minor, would have understood this clearly.

e) Those of us who are in faith and know Jesus will not be surprised or caught off guard at His Second Coming. We will rejoice and welcome Him. The Spirit and the Bride say, "Come!"

Revelation 3:4-5

a) Those who have not soiled their clothes/mantle or cloak. The covering/clothes, speaks of what is visible others regarding our faith in Jesus. The inner conditions of our heart are displayed by the life we live.

b) Jesus promises those who overcome will receive three things. We are overcomers by our new natures in Jesus Christ.

c) Walk with Him – Walking with Jesus is synonymous with being in agreement with Him and being close to Him.

d) Dressed in White – Being covered in the purity and sanctification which He imparts to His people.

e) Confessed before the Father and His angels – How wonderful it is to know that we will not be denied by Jesus! He says He would never leave us nor forsake us. He is our High Priest, Intercessor, and Deliverer.

Revelation 3:6

a) Spiritual ears are the ability hear supernatural or spiritual truth and comprehend it. Having the ability to have supernatural or spiritual senses are possible for all Christians because we are indwelt by the Holy Spirit.

Revelation 3:7

a) Words of Him who is holy and true – Greek – ALETHINOS – that which has not only the name and resemblance but also the real nature corresponding to the name, in every respect corresponding to the idea signified by the name, real, true genuine – George Eldon Ladd, in his *Commentary on the Revelation of John*, says the corresponding Hebrew thought is "One who keeps Covenant forever."

b) Jesus holds the Key of David, as He is the prophesied Branch from the root of Jesse, and is the Messianic King promised to David. Jesus' genealogy is from the Tribe of Judah, and from the House of David. It is important that the genealogy of Jesus was the ONLY genealogy that survived the destruction of the Temple because it was preserved in the Gospels of Matthew and Luke. The complete genealogy of the Tribes of Israel was destroyed by fire in AD 70 when the Temple was destroyed.

c) Jesus quotes Isaiah 22:22. The reference indicates that Jesus possesses the authority of David's Throne as Messiah. Also, in the passage, Eliakim was promoted to be father of the house of Judah over Shebna. The symbolism here is that just as there was a change in the authority to rule, Jesus is the fullness of the change as our Messianic King and High Priest. *(See Hebrews 7)*

d) Just as Eliakim had the authority to open and shut, Jesus is the ultimate authority in terms of opening and shutting. The door represents the ability to enter new spiritual opportunities and the power of the decrees of Jesus create openings for us to walk into these decrees. The Word of God - Jesus - is the Door, and His divine decrees will stand and not be overcome. This would have been very comforting to a church that was being persecuted and accused of being liars because they professed Jesus as Messiah.

Revelation 3:8

a) Jesus offers the Church of Philadelphia the promise of deliverance, as He gives them an open door into His heat for them. We all overcome through our relationship with Jesus in every time and season. This church receives no rebuke, but only promises from Jesus.

b) Jesus knows their deeds (ERGON), and understands they are on the edge of losing strength. This letter to the Philadelphian church was right on time.

c) Little power/strength – MIKROS DUNAMIS – small – strength, power, ability – In spite of the persecution they did not fall or lapse in faith.

d) Kept – Greek – TREO – to attend to carefully, take care of – to guard – These people were rooted and grounded in the Word of Christ. We are always strengthened by the Word of God. It is the very thing that is sure, unchanging, and possesses power when we anchor it in faith.

e) Deny – Greek – ARNEOMAI – to deny, to act entirely unlike himself This church lived like Sons, Priests, a Royal Nation; they did not live outside of their identity in the face of trial and persecution.

Revelation 3:9

a) The Jewish persecution of Christians in ancient Philadelphia revolved around the accusation that there were not God's people, and were Covenant Breakers.

b) Jesus endured this same persecution from the unbelieving Jews. John 8:42-44 – Jesus said to them, "If God were your Father, you would love Me, for I proceeded forth and have come from God, for I have not even come on My own initiative, but He sent Me. Why do you not understand what I am saying? It is because you cannot hear My word. You are of your father the devil, and you want to do the desires of your father. He was a murderer from the beginning, and does not stand in the truth because there is no truth in him. Whenever he speaks a lie, he speaks from his own nature, for he is a liar and the father of lies."

c) Romans 2:28-29 – For he is not a Jew who is one outwardly, nor is circumcision that which is outward in the flesh. But he is a Jew who is one inwardly; and circumcision is that which is of the heart, by the Spirit, not by the letter; and his praise is not from men, but from God.

d) Jesus was promising the Christians in Philadelphia that He would defend them and prove they were Children of God. They belonged to God because they believed He was Messiah. How wonderful it is to know Jesus is the One who defends our love for Him and will vindicate all attacks against our faith in Him!

e) Fall down and acknowledge "I have loved you" – With the destruction of the Temple in AD70, God confirmed the New Covenant, and put away the Old Covenant *(See Hebrews)*. God loves His Bride, the Church.

f) Lastly, we see a cultural play on words. Many times in the Old Testament, the Lord promised to humiliate the Gentile nations. Ezekiel 37:28; Isaiah 49:23 & Isaiah 60:14 – "The sons of those who afflicted you will come bowing to you, And all those who despised you will bow themselves at the soles of your feet; And they will call you the city of the LORD, The Zion of the Holy One of Israel.

Revelation 3:10

a) Jesus continues to commend them because they have stayed in faith and have not compromised. Not compromising in our faith is a loud trumpet blast in the spirit realm which shouts triumph and victory over the enemy. This is preaching loudly without words.

b) Jesus promises to keep them from the hour of trial. Trial – Greek – PEIRASMOS – the trial of man's fidelity, integrity, virtue, constancy

c) Trial coming to the whole world – Greek – OIKOUMEN – the civilized world – the whole of the Roman Empire at that time.

d) Those who live on the earth – Greek – GE – localized area – usually in connection with the land of Judea. *(See Matthew 24)*

e) During this era there were many trials the Church endured. There were ten persecutions against Christianity at this time. The greatest trial was the Roman invasion of Judea, and the destruction of the Temple in AD 70.

f) The practical application which applies to our times is that there is a level of faith and endurance that delivers us from mega trials! James 4:7 – Submit therefore to God. Resist the devil and he will flee from you.

Revelation 3:11

a) Coming soon – Greek – ERCHOMAI – Verb – to come

b) This is not a reference to Jesus' Second Coming. He is simply stating He will come to them soon and deliver them from the trial. That is the context of this encouragement from Jesus.

c) Jesus Christ will return – Acts 1:11 – They also said, "Men of Galilee, why do you stand looking into the sky? This Jesus, who has been taken up from you into heaven, will come in just the same way as you have watched Him go into heaven." *(See Revelation 21 & Revelation 22)*

d) The church of Philadelphia had been given crowns – Greek – STEPHANOS – a crown or a mark of royalty (in general) exalted rank. Beloved, we are crowned with His glory, love, grace and blessing because we are a Royal Priesthood. *(See 1 Peter 2:9)*

e) Kingdom kids cannot be paupers or beggars because we bear the mark of Kingdom Royalty! Understanding our identity in Jesus will strength us to receive the promises of God. We can only pray and intercede according to our knowledge of God and the measure of faith we possess.

Revelation 3:12-13

a) The one who overcomes will receive four promises.

b) Pillar in the Temple of God – 1 Kings 7:21 – Thus he set up the pillars at the porch of the nave; and he set up the right pillar and named it Jachin, and he set up the left pillar and named it Boaz. Jachin means *He will establish*. Boaz means *fleetness, swift or rapid; to cause or to pass swiftly; to fly*

c) Name of My God – Yahweh – Those who have been given the Name implies close relationship with the Father. This is the Covenant Name of God.

d) Name of the City of My God – New Jerusalem – The natural Jerusalem was going to be destroyed soon, as it was a shadow of a greater reality in which God would dwell with mankind first in the Person of the Holy Spirit, and then in full blown manifestation at Jesus' Second Coming. *(See Revelation 21)*

e) Jesus' New Name – Revelation 19:16 – KING OF KINGS AND LORD OF LORDS

f) He who has an ear, let him hear – Hebrews 5:14 – But solid food is for the mature, who because of practice have their senses trained to discern good and evil.

g) Beloved, the more we invest our hearts into His heart we gain the ability to have our spiritual senses heightened!

Revelation 3:14

a) The words of the AMEN – Surely, truly or of a truth – Vines Dictionary Comments: The word "amen" is a most remarkable word. It was transliterated directly from the Hebrew into the Greek of the New Testament, then into Latin and into English and many other languages, so that it is practically a universal word. It has been called the best known word in human speech. The word is directly related — in fact, almost identical — to the Hebrew word for "believe" (amam), or faithful. Thus, it came to mean "sure" or "truly", an expression of absolute trust and confidence – Jesus can be absolutely trusted and the Word of His mouth is pure VERITAS.

b) Faithful and true witness – Jesus is faithful in representing the heart of Father. Jesus is faithful in obeying the Law, as He is the Word made flesh. Jesus was faithful to obey the Father and endure the sufferings of the cross. Jesus was faithful to demonstrate the Kingdom of God and the manifestation of its rule by healing the sick, raising the dead, casting out demons, teaching its truth and showing mercy to those in sin.

c) Ruler of God's creation – Matthew 28:18-20 – All authority has been given to Jesus on heaven and on earth. At His Name every knee will bow and every tongue will confess He is Lord. I believe sometimes we discount the authority that Jesus possesses, therefore robbing ourselves of the benefits of the Kingdom that are rightfully ours as heirs of the Kingdom and Children of God.

d) Jesus is addressing this church with the full authority of the One whose Word carries finality and power.

Revelation 3:15-16

a) This is a play on words. The water supply of Laodicea was from a hot spring about 5 miles south of the city. Archaeologists have mapped the aqueduct and determined the water must have been very hard, and lukewarm by the time it reached the city. The Greek geographer, Strabo, noted the water was "very hard, but drinkable."

b) Jesus uses the play on words to describe the spiritual condition of their deeds. The Greek word for deeds – ERGON – that which one is employed by, or business, or that which one undertakes to do – This church was lacking in the area of authenticity in worship and faith works.

c) Jesus used the metaphor of spitting them out – Greek – EMEO – to vomit – Worship that is feigned and faith works with no action do not minister to Jesus. Romans 12 describes the sacrifices of the Beloved in Jesus, as being holy and pleasing to Him. *(See Romans 12:1-3)*

Revelation 3:17-18

a) The Church at Laodicea had tremendous wealth and resources compared to the other six churches of the region. Their attitude was one of self-dependence and not dependence upon Jesus. The charge was that they declared they did "not need a thing". We can have tremendous blessing and prosperity and be thankful and dependent on Jesus. Jesus is not preaching poverty to the Laodiceans, but dependence.

b) We have the second play on words in verse 17. The medical school in Laodicea was famous for Coryllium, an eye salve that was used to heal the eyes from disease. Apparently, this church had no anointing of illumination and revelation. *(See Ephesians 1:18-23)*

c) In Christ we are forgiven, covered, provided for, blessed, loved, and benefited in amazing ways. The denial of these truths by this church left them in spiritual lack. They were becoming spiritually bankrupt by denying their need for Jesus and their lack of intimacy in loving Him.

d) The third play on words is regarding them being naked. Laodicea was famous for producing beautiful black wool that was used for fine clothing. Jesus offers them white clothes as symbols of the purity they can have in Him.

e) Jesus possess the wealth that makes people prosperous in soul. Gold refined in the fire is a metaphor for the wealth of revelation that comes from the Flame of God, the Holy Spirit. Fire is also a metaphor for the passion of God, and His flaming heart of love for His people. Jesus wants this church to know Him passionately.

Revelation 3:19

a) Those I love – PHILEO – Greek – to love, approve of, to like, to sanction, to treat kindly, or affectionately, to welcome, to befriend, to show signs of love, to kiss, to be fond of doing, to be wanted – Jesus loves us too much to abandon us to a wayward path.

b) Hebrews 12:10-11 – The discipline of God is NOT God creating tragedies, illness and calamities as means of bringing us back to Him. The root word for discipline here is Greek – PAIDEIA – the whole training and education of a child including moral training, cultivation of the mind, moral correction and admonition, and the care of the body. No parent uses evil to teach and train children. That is a crime called *child abuse!*

c) We can expect the Lord to train us to become like Himself. Jesus asks the Laodicean church to be zealous – Greek – ZELEUO- to be jealous or full of zeal. To repent – to change one's mind!

d) The believer in Christ can make a decision of the heart to be taught by God, the most loving, kind, forgiving, merciful, and gracious Being, the One in whom there is no darkness at all.

Revelation 3:20

a) Jesus stands at the door of the heart and knocks. The Laodicean Church is being offered the first of two amazing promises for repentance.

b) Jesus would dine with us – A metaphor for intimate friendship. What is it like to feast on Jesus and be nourished by what He gives us? He is the Bread of Life and the Living Water!

Revelation 3:21

a) This is the second amazing promise – Jesus will give us the grace of authority and the grace to sit on the throne with Him. Ephesians 2:6 & Colossians 3:1 teach we are seated with Christ in heavenly realms.

b) Being seated with Christ also means we are resting in His finished work of salvation. Jesus completed all that was necessary in terms of obtaining salvation for the whole world. He is seated in holy authority and ruling power over everything. Romans 8 says we are more than conquerors, and inseparable from His love, when we are resting in Christ.

Revelation 3:22

a) Every believer in Jesus Christ is equipped to hear what the Spirit says as we have the Holy Spirit residing in us. Through the Holy Spirit we have access to see and hear what God communicates to us.

CHAPTER FOUR

In Revelation Chapter Four, we will step into John's second prophetic vision into the Throne Room/Realm of God the Father. We will be introduced to the majesty and beauty of God and the diversity of the angelic created order. We will be inspired to worship God in more depth and intensity by John's second vision.

The purpose of the second vision is to communicate truth about God in terms of His eternal nature, and Him being above all things and worthy of all worship. This would have been a strong encouragement to the Early Church who was facing persecutions and challenges all around them. It is also an encouragement to every generation of believers in Jesus Christ and an inspiration for us to worship our God with same passion as the angelic order in this chapter.

Revelation 4:1

a) The door open in heaven is the door of revelation that John, the Beloved, would go through to see realms of God's revelation and illumination. Doors in Scripture represent moments of opportunity between God and people. We call these moments *KAIROS* moments. These are times of convergence where we move from one season to another. Because the door is located in heaven, we can assume from the text that John is in another trance state after having received the Letters to the Seven Churches.

b) John was invited to "come up here" by a loud voice like a trumpet. In Revelation 1:10, the voice of Jesus was described as a "like a loud trumpet." We can see Jesus is still speaking to John in this second prophetic vision by the phrase, "the voice I had first heard speaking to me". Jesus is the access to realms of revelation and experiential knowledge, as He is the door for the sheep to enter in. It is through Jesus that we access all of the forgiveness, blessing, mercy, love and grace of God. In verse 1, we see the Holy Spirit and Jesus in unity bringing the second vision to John. The book of Revelation is distinctly Trinitarian.

c) What takes place after this – This is what takes place after the Letters to the Seven Churches. The Church of Jesus Christ is only about 30-40 years old at this point in salvation history. The Lord needed to encourage His Body into the wonderful destiny they would walk out as they destroy the works of the devil, and bring the dominion of God's Kingdom to the world by preaching the Gospel. We are still engaged in this same call and destiny! The Church will continue to be encouraged by this wonderful prophetic book. The First Century Church was small and weak, having just been born, but they were empowered by the Holy Spirit. They were facing persecutions by the Jews and Romans, and they needed the prophetic visions of the Revelation to give them grace to grow strong and prosper in their high calling in Jesus as revolutionary World Changers. The whole world has profited by the presence of the Church.

Revelation 4:2-3

a) The One who sat on the throne in heaven – Greek – OURANOS – the region above the natural heavens, the seat of order of things eternal and consummately perfect where God dwells and other heavenly beings – God being seated communicates to us that God is at rest and in the fullness of peace. He does not need to work His will; He only needs to decree His will!

b) Despite the condition of the world, God dwells as King and Lord. We can be comforted to know that God is above all things and before all things.

c) No anthropomorphism is given to God in this vision. He is only described as having the appearance of Jasper and Carnelian. This is an invitation for us to think of God according to the symbolism of the two gem stones given to us in this vision.

d) Jasper – Red in color – This symbolizes the passion, desire, emotion, and the love of God. 1 John 4:8 says that God is love. In the color red, we see the symbolism of the passionate red redemptive blood of Jesus, and fullness of who God is at the very essence of His being.

e) Carnelian – Orange in color – Hebrews 12:29 says our God is a Consuming Fire. This is symbolic language for the intensity of His being, the coming fires of judgment at the end of the New Covenant Age, and the purity of the flame of His heart that refines those He loves.

f) Rainbow resembling an emerald – We have two symbols to interpret here: The rainbow symbolizes God's never changing Word and Covenant promises to His people. The emerald is a green stone and is transparent. An emerald rainbow symbolizes the life of God extended to those who are in Covenant with Him. It encircles His throne because a circle has no beginning or end. God is eternal, and His Word and Covenant are forever.

Revelation 4:4

a) The 24 thrones and 24 elders surrounding the Throne of God are angelic beings who sit in the counsel and wisdom of God.

b) They are wearing white, the raiment of angels – Angels are described as wearing white in John 20:12, Matthew 28:3, Acts 1:10, Mark 16:5 – Paul describes a multitude of angelic ranks in

Colossians 1:16, Romans 8:38, and Ephesians 3:10.

c) Many OT verses describe God as being surrounded, or in the presence of the angelic order. *(See Psalm 89:7, Isaiah 24:23, 1 Kings 22:19)*

d) These angelic elders have the angelic functions of worship, enforcing God's decrees as they sit on thrones, and wear gold crowns.

e) Through this prophetic vision, we are given the invitation to participate in it with a holy imagination being inspired by the Holy Spirit.

Revelation 4:5

a) From the throne came thundering and lightning - These are common manifestations of the power and presence of God in Scripture. *(See Exodus 19:16, Ezekiel 1:13)* These symbolize the power, authority, suddenness, and glory of the presence of God. *(See Psalm 18:13-15 & Job 37:2-5)*

b) Nothing compares to power and authority, and swiftness of His Word. From this throne all of purposes of life and destiny are spoken.

c) The Sevenfold Spirit or Seven Spirits of God - This is symbolic language for the perfection of the Holy Spirit, with seven being the number of perfection or of being complete. What we have here is the typical type and shadow used as description of the Holy Spirit. This type of allegory or symbolism is used throughout the Revelation. *(See Isaiah 11:1-3)*

Revelation 4:6

a) The Sea of Glass/Crystal - This symbolizes the purity of God and His holiness. God is perfectly pure, holy and good. Our view of God should be filtered through these truths.

b) There was a Bronze Sea/Laver before the Old Testament altar where the priests would wash before serving before the Lord (1 Kings 7:23-26 & 2 Chronicles 4:2-6). As believers, we have been made pure by the Lord Jesus, and we are priests before Him, and can approach Him on this Sea of purity and holiness. In this vision, we see the real Sea as the Sea of the Temple which was only a shadow of the greater reality in heaven.

c) We can also connect this Sea to the visions in Exodus 24:10 & Ezekiel 1:22; 26. It is important to keep in mind that Revelation parallels the Old Testament imagery of Isaiah, Ezekiel, Joel, Zechariah, and Psalms. It should be interpreted according to the context of this imagery.

d) The four living creatures are analogous to Ezekiel's vision in Ezekiel 1 and Isaiah's vision in Isaiah 6. The reference to these creatures having been covered with eyes communicates to us that these creatures were created to see the fullness of God's beauty and their ceaseless vigilance in declaring His praise. Their position being mentioned in the center and around the throne can be interpreted that they are under God's throne mediating His divine power and energy to the world. The created angelic order possesses a diversity that mirrors God's created natural order.

Revelation 4:8-9

a) From very early times in Church history, the faces of the four creatures have been connected to the four Gospels and their various points of view in their portrayal of Jesus. The natural interpretation in the text does not support that view. However, the face of each living creature communicates to us something about their angelic function.

b) The face of a lion – The symbol of courage, bravery, and fierceness in battle.

c) The face of an ox – The symbol of power, service and faithfulness in labor.

d) The face of man – The symbol of being created in God's image and the crown of His created order.

e) The face of an eagle – The symbol of powerful flight and the safety of the heights on which eagles fly. This can also symbolize having prophetic vision and revelation.

f) We can summarize that the totality of the four faces represent the fullness of these creatures' callings and heavenly assignments. These are very powerful and wonderful creatures who declare the praise of the Living God in their song.

g) "Holy, holy, holy is the Lord God Almighty, who was, and is and is to come." The never-ending song is never ending because it declares the infinity of God and His everlasting and eternal Being. This is an expression of "I AM." It is comforting to know the God we worship, possesses inexhaustible qualities, character and mystery.

Revelation 4:10-11

a) The 24 elders reciprocate and declare what the creatures say is true. They are the Amen to the creatures' song.

b) Worthy – Greek AXIOUS – weighing, having weight, having the weight of another thing of like value, worth as much – The Lord is worthy above all things to be praised as He is Creator God.

c) Glory – Greek – DOXA – opinion of something, magnificence, excellence, preeminence, dignity, grace, the kingly majesty which belongs to him as Supreme Ruler, majesty in the sense of the absolute perfection of the Deity.

d) Honor – Greek – TIM – a valuing by which the price is fixed, of the honor which one has by reason of rank and state of office which he holds, deference, reverence.

e) Power – Greek – DYNAMIS – strength power, ability, inherent power, power residing in a thing by virtue of its nature, or which a person or thing exerts and puts forth.

f) The declarative song of the elders also teaches us that creation was first in God's mind and then came to being by His will. It is God bringing forth something from nothing, which is the ultimate display of power and authority.

g) This amazing vision of God, which Jesus invited John through the door to experience, empowered and strengthened the First Century Church to endure the spiritual warfare that was being waged against them as they expanded the rule and reign of this beautiful Creator God. This vision today continues to inspire the Modern Church to worship, praise and be strengthened in the times in which we live.

CHAPTER FIVE

Revelation Chapter Five continues John's trance/ecstatic state vision of the Throne Room in heaven. We see Jesus becoming the center of attention in heaven as He takes the seven sealed scroll. This chapter is full of awesome symbolism and prophetic revelation of Jesus Christ.

In the context of being a First Century believer who would have received the Revelation, Chapter Five would have continued to be a source of encouragement to a theologically immature, weak, and persecuted church. This chapter would have also been the source of inspired worship and adoration of Jesus to them and to us.

As we look at the whole of Chapter Five, we are presented with a wide panoramic view of the whole of salvation history. This is a very significant chapter as it holds the keys that outline the rest of this prophetic book. The remainder of the Revelation is the re-telling of the story of the victorious Messiah: Jesus and the extension of His rule which ultimately ushers in His visible eternal rule on earth. We see the re-telling of the account of the rule and reign of Jesus in the geopolitical context of the Roman Empire, the destruction of Judea, and in the supernatural context of the spiritual warfare that is waged as the Kingdom of God is expanded through the Church.

The conclusion of Chapter Five would have left the First Century hearer of the Revelation encouraged and strengthened to believe in the success of the Messiah and His Church. The Church in Chapter Five is being rooted in its identity as the people of God.

Revelation 5:1

a) God the Father is on the throne and possesses the "Title Deed" to the redemption of all things.

b) The scroll with writing on both sides and sealed with seven seals is significant. In ancient times, a sealed document indicated an authoritative and important document. It could only be opened by the one authorized to open the seals.

c) The number 7 in Scripture is the number of completeness, fullness, perfection, or finished works.

d) The identity of the one who could open the scroll is hinted to us in Revelation 1:1 – The Revelation of Jesus Christ, which God gave Him to show to His bond-servants, the things which must soon take place; and He sent and communicated it by His angel to His bond-servant John. Since the Revelation is a *revelation*, Jesus would be One who would be able to reveal the contents of the scroll to His people. A vast portion of this prophetic book revolves around the opening of the seals. We can see from the very start of this book we are interpreting the book by understanding its symbolism in the context of the culture, historical events that actually happened that prove the Revelation and our faith is true, and allowing the Scriptures to interpret Scripture.

e) We see a foreshadowing of this scroll in Daniel 12:4 – But as for you, Daniel, conceal these words and seal up the book until the end of time; many will go back and forth, and knowledge will increase. – Later, Daniel began to ask about the sealed book and God answered him in Daniel 12:7 – I heard the man dressed in linen, who was above the waters of the river, as he raised his right hand and his left toward heaven, and swore by Him who lives forever that it would be for a time, times, and half a time; and as soon as they finish shattering the power of the holy people, all these events will be completed. – This prophecy was fulfilled in AD70 when the destruction of Jerusalem was completed after a 3.5 year siege. I mention this because most of the apocalyptic prophecy of the Old Testament and the apocalyptic prophecies of Jesus were fulfilled in the times when Jerusalem was destroyed in AD70.

Revelation 5:2

a) In this verse, we continue to see the diversity of the angelic order that God created. Apparently, this angel was "mighty/strong", characterizing his rank and assignment.

b) Loud voice – MEGAS PHONE – Greek – used of intensity and its degrees: with great effort, of the affections and emotions of the mind, of natural events powerfully affecting the senses: violent, mighty, strong – a sound or tone, of instruments, of uttered voices.

c) Who is worthy – This is the charge. The Only One worthy would be the One who could pay the price for the "Title Deed" of redemption. Jesus being the Second Adam, who did not fail into temptation, who was perfect and without sin, who was obedient to the Father, and defeated death and hell, would be worthy.

Revelation 5:3-4

a) No created being was found worthy to possess the scroll of the redemption of all things.

b) There is a theological concept here that Mankind is not worthy to save itself nor capable to work it out.

c) The second theological concept here is that only One co-equal with the Father would be worthy. This points us to the divinity of Jesus Christ as the God-Man.

d) John wept – John was still having his theology of Jesus formed, because he wept tears of hopelessness regarding the redemption. This would have been terribly discouraging as he is witnessing this vision in his trance state.

Revelation 5:5

a) One of the elders – This would have been one of the 24 angelic elders around the throne.

b) Do not weep – Jesus is the Daystar rising in our hearts. The weeping may last for the night, but joy comes in the morning. A revelation of Jesus ends all weeping and brings hope.

c) The Elder Angel points John to specific prophecies about the Person of Jesus.

d) Lion of the Tribe of Judah and the Root of David – Isaiah 11:1 – Then a shoot will spring from the stem of Jesse, And a branch from his roots will bear fruit. Micah 5:2 – But as for you, Bethlehem Ephrathah, Too little to be among the clans of Judah, From you One will go forth for Me to be ruler in Israel. His goings forth are from long ago, From the days of eternity. Isaiah 65:9 – I will bring forth offspring from Jacob, And an heir of My mountains from Judah; Even My chosen ones shall inherit it, And My servants will dwell there. Genesis 49:9 – Judah is a lion's whelp; From the prey, my son, you have gone up. He crouches, he lies down as a lion, And as a lion, who dares rouse him up? Genesis 49:10 – The scepter shall not depart from Judah, Nor the ruler's staff from between his feet, until Shiloh comes, And to him shall be the obedience of the peoples.

e) He has triumphed – Greek – NIKA – to conquer, to carry off the victory, come off victorious – Jesus defeated Satan and demons and all the evil resident in their realm by His death and resurrection. Colossians 2:15 – When He had disarmed the rulers and authorities, He made a public display of them, having triumphed over them through Him. Colossians 2:14 says that Jesus defeated the judgment that we were to receive as Law breakers by His death on the cross. It is important to know that Jesus worked a victory that we could have never worked. We triumph with Him because we are in Him!

f) He is able – Greek – ANOIG – verb – to open – Jesus opens all the doors of revelation and illumination and shows His people. Psalm 25:14 – The secret of the LORD is for those who fear Him, And He will make them know His covenant.

Revelation 5:6

a) In chapter 4, we mentioned the significance of the place where the 4 living creatures were positioned. They were under and around the throne. From this language, we conclude they were around and centered directly under the throne. Jesus proceeds from the very center of the throne. This symbolism shows that Jesus proceeds forth from the Father. Galatians 4:4 – But when the fullness of the time came, God sent forth His Son.

b) The Lamb, who is a Lion – Slain – Greek – SPHAZ – to slay, slaughter, butcher – to put to death by violence – mortally wounded – Jesus was a Lamb in terms of His innocence and sacrifice; He was a Lion in terms of His courage, strength and obedience to the Father as He endured the torture of the cross for the justification of our sins. The marks of His suffering are eternal and speak of the everlasting salvation He worked.

c) Jesus is the center of attention and all the angelic order worships Him and praises Him. He is the center of our attention as well and we are a loving Bride who longs for the Bridegroom.

d) Seven horns – This speaks of the absolute authority of Jesus as the One worthy to take the scroll.

e) Seven eyes – Jesus has intense passion and desire, omnipotence, omnipresence, and His eyes burn with prefect vision in regards to all things. These are further attributes of His deity as the

Second Person of the Trinity. The fourth and fifth chapters of Revelation are full of Trinitarian theology.

Revelation 5:7

a) Only Jesus could take the scroll from the right hand of the Father. The right hand in Scripture symbolizes power, authority, omnipotence, strength, and the power to rule.

Revelation 5:8

a) When Jesus takes the scroll, the attention of heaven is focused on Him and the creatures and elders who were worshiping the One on the throne, begin to worship the Lamb. This is a clear indication Jesus is worthy of worship and divine; He is a God-Man.

b) Each one had a harp – Greek – KITHARA – a harp which praises of God are sung in heaven – This is a very interesting word as it is has no known root word, and is always in the context of being used in heaven. It not an earthly instrument, but a heavenly one. To sing the song of heaven, it must be revealed to one by heaven. Here is worship being a vehicle of prophetic spontaneous song as the elders and creatures play the KITHARA and worship the Lamb.

c) Bowls of incense – It is a wonderful symbol of our prayers being a sweet-smelling sacrifice to the Lord. We can offer no other sacrifice than to spend ourselves in thankful worship and in petition of prayer. God enjoys our prayers and the godly meditations of our hearts. They are found in the hands of the very closest spiritual beings in heaven, in the form of golden bowls full of incense.

d) Gold in Scripture represents power, wealth, and things having eternal value. Our prayers have worth and eternal value. Verse 8 says the bowls are full. This is symbolism that God does not lightly esteem the prayers of His people. The word for bowls in the Greek indicate that the bowls are large deep, saucers, made of gold, being full.

e) Prayers of the saints – Greek – HAGIOS – most holy thing, a saint – It is truly amazing that despite all of our weaknesses and spiritual immaturity, we are regarded as most holy people

Revelation 5:9

a) A new song – This song has never been sung before in heaven. What we are seeing in verses 9-14 is a wide panoramic view of the totality of the redemption Jesus Christ accomplished by His death and resurrection. Greek – KAINOS – new, recently made, fresh, recent, unused, unworn Greek – ODE – song or ode.

b) Jesus is being worshiped in heaven – we continue to see the divine nature in Christ as the Second Person of the Godhead.

c) The atonement of Jesus is presented to us in Verse 9 as being much wider than the redemption of Israel. The concept of Messiah is for the whole world, not just the believing remnant of Israel who accepted Jesus as Messiah. This section of Chapter Five is a wide view of the whole of redemption history. The churches receiving the Revelation were still small, persecuted by Jews and Romans, and struggling in their theology. Hearing this new song would have encouraged the early church in its destiny. The new song should encourage us as well.

d) Purchased – Greek – AGORAZ – to be in the market place, to attend it – Just as Adam and Eve sold humanity to death and subjected creation to the influence of Satan and his inferior influence, Jesus Christ purchased the Title Deed of Redemption (the scroll), by His blood. The Greek word is a verb, and Jesus worked a salvation available to the whole world that we are not capable of working or paying for ourselves. As we come to Jesus Christ, we are bond servants who are grateful for His love, compassion and grace. The one who has been forgiven much, loves much. We were purchased for God. The Godhead sees us in the light of having the worth to work a salvation that we might be His own possession.

Revelation 5:10

a) God's people are a kingdom. Christ rules in the hearts of His people and His rule and reign extend through us, the collective body of the Church. 1 Peter 2:9 – But you are A CHOSEN RACE, a ROYAL PRIESTHOOD, A HOLY NATION, A PEOPLE FOR God's OWN POSSESSION, so that you may proclaim the excellencies of Him who has called you out of darkness into His marvelous light. Jesus said the Kingdom of God is within us.

b) Priests – Greek – HIEREUS – a priest, one who offers sacrifices and in general, busied with sacred rites – We offer the sacrifices of worship, thankfulness and praise. Romans 12 – Priests also represent the God they serve. As the Church of Jesus Christ, we model His nature and character. We display the rule and reign of Jesus in our ministry and lives.

c) This verse teaches us the Church is ruling and reigning spiritually, and we are in the position of authority to extend the rule of Jesus in the earth. These verses do not present us as being anemic and weak, but presents us being powerful and having dominion with Christ. The true destiny of God's people is much more positive than many of us believe to be true. Our experience should never define our faith. Our faith in what is true should shape our present reality.

Revelation 5:11

a) All of heavens' attention was directed to Jesus, the Lamb who was slain. We have a view of the angelic hosts who love and serve the Lord of Hosts.

b) We can see the passion of the angels in their song extolling the great virtue and majesty of Jesus.

c) The ten thousand times ten thousand language is symbolic of an innumerable assembly of heavenly hosts. There are more angels in the service and worship of God than demons who fell. Greek – MYRIAS – an innumerable multitude, an unlimited number. Revelation 12:4 says a third of the stars fell with the dragon. The stars are fallen angels, the dragon is Satan.

Revelation 5:12

a) Worthy – Greek – AXIOS – weighing, having weight, having the weight of another thing of like value, worth as much – Jesus possesses the weight of glory, and greatness of His redemption. There is no one found worthy except Jesus to receive the scroll of redemption and the destiny of creation.

b) Power – Greek – DYNAMIS – strength power, ability, inherent power, power residing in a thing by virtue of its nature, or which a person or thing exerts and puts forth; power for performing miracles; moral power and excellence of soul; the power and influence which belong to riches and wealth; power and resources arising from numbers; power consisting in or resting upon armies, forces, hosts

c) Wealth – Greek – PLOUTOS – riches, wealth – abundance of external possessions – fullness, abundance, plenitude

d) Wisdom – Greek – SOPHIA – wisdom, broad and full of intelligence; used of the knowledge of very diverse matters, the varied knowledge of things human and divine, acquired by acuteness and experience, and summed up in maxims and proverbs – the science of learning – the intelligence evinced in discovering the meaning of some mysterious number or vision, supreme intelligence, such as belongs to God – the wisdom of God as evinced in forming and executing counsels in the formation and government of the world and the scriptures

e) Strength or Might – Greek – ISCHYS – ability, force, strength, might

f) Honor – Greek – TIME – a valuing by which the price is fixed – of the honor which one has by reason of rank and state of office which he holds.

g) Glory – Greek – DOXA – the kingly majesty which belongs to him as Supreme Ruler, majesty in the sense of the absolute perfection of the deity.

h) Praise – Greek – EULOGIA – praise, laudation, panegyric: of Christ or God.

i) Jesus has received these things as the victorious Messiah. As God's people, we can receive from Jesus the greatness of all of these things in a measure of faith. The language of verse 12 is to provoke us to worship this truly awesome Savior.

Revelation 5:13

a) Every creature – Greek – KTISMA – thing founded; created thing – Romans 8:20-22 teaches us that all creation was subject to frustration by Adam through the Fall of Man. This means creation is out of its original intent and suffering the effects of sin , just as humanity suffers the effects of the Fall. KTISMA would also include the whole of humanity.

b) Jesus is the Restorer of the created order. At the Second Coming of Jesus, the Restored Order of all things will be established.

c) The whole of Revelation Chapter Five is a wide panoramic view of the whole of salvation history. The remainder of Revelation is the re-telling of salvation history multiple times, showing the story in a multitude of views from the historical geopolitical context of the Roman Empire to the supernatural warfare being waged as the Kingdom of God with the salvation and redemption of the whole of creation that is obtained by Jesus.

Revelation 5:14

a) The intimate hosts of the four living creatures and the 24 elders "Amen" or agree and worship of the Lamb. Romans 14:11-12 - Every knee will bow, every tongue confess – Chapter Five ends with the entirety of heaven with all creation bowing and confessing Jesus Christ.

CHAPTER SIX

In Chapter Six, Jesus begins to open the seals of the scroll He received from the Father. It is important to note that Jesus received the Scroll of the Redemption of all creation. Through the process of opening the Seals, we see Jesus revealing the whole story of the conflict and conquest of Redemption History.

The opening of the Seven Seals to the Pouring Out of the Seven Bowls are basically the same narrative, told in increasing degrees of intensity. This understanding of Revelation will greatly simplify and demystify the book of Revelation, pointing us to the historical context of the Revelation. Revelation Chapter 1 tells us the things that are to be revealed in this prophetic book are "near/soon". So, the best way to understand the book is in the context of the First Century Early Church and the geopolitical struggles that surrounded them at the time.

Our main source material for interpreting the Seven Seals and Seven Trumpets are the "first mentions" in the Old Testament, Josephus' Histories, and Early Church History. Our approach to the Revelation is from the Classic Partial Preterist View which is has been a prominent view in the Church for 2000 years, and supported by world history.

As we begin Chapter Six, John's trance/vision continues in its intensity as he witnesses the playing out of Redemption History. We then conclude Revelation Chapter Six, seeing how this New Testament prophetic letter to the First Century Church was fulfilled in history. To the churches receiving the Revelation, this prophetic vision given to

John would have comforted them and encouraged them during the persecutions and hardships they were facing.

It is important to demystify the book of Revelation and interpret it in the context of the First Century, what Jesus prophesied in Matthew 24 and the history surrounding the fall of Jerusalem in AD 70.

What we believe about the future flavors the way we live our lives, minister to others, and our outlook regarding our destinies or life paths.

Revelation 6:1

a) John receives the invitation from one of the four living creatures, to come and see the opening of the Seals so that he can report to the Seven Churches what is about to take place in the world around them.

b) The voice of the creature is described to us as "thunder". Thunder in Scripture speaks of the power of God, the Judgment of God, and sudden fulfillment of God's words. *(See Exodus 9:23, 1 Samuel 7:10, 1 Samuel 12:18, Job 40:9, Isaiah 29:6, Psalm 77:18)*

c) It is important for us to keep in mind that the Seals are opened by Jesus Christ. Jesus is in charge of the whole of world history because all authority has been given to Him, in heaven and on earth. It is error for us to impute that Satan is managing the Revelation or somehow dictating the terms of the judgment we are reading about in the opening of the Seven Seals and the Seven Trumpets.

d) In the opening of the Seven Seals we see the progressive panoramic view of the struggle between the Kingdom of God and the inferior dominion of Satan.

Revelation 6:2

a) We are introduced to the Rider on the White Horse. The natural interpretation of the identity of the Rider is found in Revelation 19:11-16.

b) White – Symbol of Purity and Holiness

c) Bow – Symbol of warfare, swift judgment and power, or bow of God *(See Psalm 7:12, Isaiah 41:2, Lamentations 2:4, Zechariah 9:3)*

d) Crown – Jesus is King of Kings and Lord of Lords. Jesus is crowned with honor and glory.

e) Jesus Christ is a conquering King by means of the authority of the Gospel, and the spiritual domination of the Church over the forces of evil. Jesus is bent on conquest, because He is in the process of the violent overthrow from the effects of the Fall. He has passion to accomplish the cause of His suffering on the cross.

f) The city of Jerusalem is also in view, because Jesus told the Sanhedrin that they would see Him come in power and mourn their decision for rejecting Him and crucifying Him. *(See Matthew 26:64)* Jesus also comes as Judge who removes the Temple (AD 70) and establishes His Church. Matthew 27:25 – All the people answered, "Let his blood be on us and on our children."

Revelation 6:3-4

a) The second Living Creature invites John to witness the opening of the Second Seal.

b) The symbolism of the Fiery Red Horse shows us the nature of its mission. Red is used to symbolize the destructive nature of the devil, and the attitude of hatred and warfare. The red horse is the Roman Army and their destruction of the land of Judea and Jerusalem.

c) The mission of its rider was to take peace away from the land (earth). The Greek word for land is GE – It commonly means a local geographic area rather than the entirety of the planet. (Compare with OIKOUMENE – known civilized world). Matthew 24, will help us understand the opening of the Seven Seals. In Matthew 24, Jesus prophesied the complete destruction of Jerusalem and the Temple within the time frame of one generation. The content of Matthew 24 parallels Revelation Chapter Six.

d) The one who fulfilled the Second Seal mission was Vespasian and his son, Titus. Josephus, being an eye witness to the Roman military invasion of Judea and the Siege of Jerusalem, gives us a detailed account of the mass scale of murder, bloodshed and warfare the Roman army carried out against the Jewish nation who rejected Jesus as Messiah.

e) We are not waiting for a Fiery Red Horse to be loosed in our times as Jesus judged sinful Jerusalem, and removed the Temple because its purpose was fulfilled when the New Covenant was established.

Revelation 6:5-6

a) The third living creature invites John to witness the effects of the Third Seal that Jesus opens.

b) During the Roman siege of Jerusalem, Josephus describes in great detail the horrors of the famine in Jerusalem. "So all hope of escaping was now cut off from the Jews, together with their liberty of going out of the city. Then did the famine widen its progress, and devoured the people by whole houses and families; the upper rooms were full of women and children that were dying by famine, and the lanes of the city were full of the dead bodies of the aged; the children also and the young men wandered about the market-places like shadows, all swelled with the famine, and fell down dead, wheresoever their misery seized them. As for burying them, those that were sick themselves were not able to do it; and those that were hearty and well were deterred from doing it by the great multitude of those dead bodies, and by the uncertainty there was how soon they should die themselves; for many died as they were burying others, and many went to their coffins before that fatal hour was come."

c) Josephus writes an account of a mother eating her child, and the cost of wheat and grain being extremely high during the siege of Jerusalem. It is well worth our time to read about the accuracy of Jesus' words in Matthew 24, in the account that Josephus documents in his Histories of the Jews.

d) Josephus mentions this account of John Levi swallowing up the oil and wine of the Temple. At this time, he and his rebels were living in and plundering the Temple. "While they were fighting for the Divinity, without fear, and that such whose warfare is for the temple should live of the temple; on which account he emptied the vessels of that sacred wine and oil, which the priests kept to be poured on the burnt-offerings, and which lay in the inner court of the temple, and distributed it among the multitude, who, in their anointing themselves and drinking, used [each of them] above an hin of them."

Revelation 6:7-8

a) The Lamb – The Redemptive Identity of Jesus Christ as the perfect sacrifice for the sins of all.

b) The fourth living creature invites John to witness the contents of the opening of the Fourth Seal. Keep in mind the land (GE) is concerning a localized area.

c) The identity of the Pale Horse or Green Horse – Greek – CHL ROS – green, yellow green pale of death. The Pale Horse is Death. Death is the fruit of sin. A portion of the Jewish nation rejected Jesus Christ and suffered the cost for rejecting the One the Father loved, who gave them their salvation. Death and Hades are destiny for everyone who does not receive Messiah.

d) In Mathew 23 and Luke 13, Jesus prophesies Jerusalem would be left desolate for rejecting Him as Messiah.

e) Josephus documents the rebel factions in Jerusalem not only killed each other, but also killed and robbed the population of people who were shut in Jerusalem. He also documents many died from famine and disease associated with not being able to remove the dead bodies from the city.

f) Number of prisoners taken in the entire war: 97,000. Number of Jews who died during the siege: 1,100,000. This large number during the siege was due to the Passover celebration, as Jews from many countries had been in the city for the festival when the siege began. Josephus tells skeptical readers this number is consistent with Cestius' population estimate under Nero.

g) Deuteronomy 28:13-68 has a detailed list of punishments for the Jewish nation being rebellious against God.

h) Early Church history tells us that not one Christian was killed during the siege of Jerusalem. There are many accounts written about the whole Christian Community who fled to Pella just before the Roman Siege. Eusebius: The first clear reference comes from the fourth century church historian Eusebius. He says that as the Romans approached the city, "The people belonging to the church at Jerusalem had been ordered by an oracle revealed to approved men on the spot before the war broke out, to leave the city and dwell in a town of Peraea called Pella" (EH III:5). *(See Matthew 24:8)*

i) Beloved, we are not waiting for mass death to come to planet earth as part of God's redemptive plan for mankind. This mindset robs the Church of her mission, and denies the grace of the New Covenant. Jesus came to give eternal and abundant life to the world.

Revelation 6:9

a) The Fifth Seal introduces us to the martyrs who have been persecuted and killed because of the Word of God and their Testimony. The Word of God being mentioned here is the Gospel of Jesus Christ, specifically that Jesus is Messiah. Their testimony is their death confession of fidelity to Him.

b) As we learned in Chapters 2-3, the Early Church was persecuted by the Roman Authorities *and* the Jews who rejected Jesus. They considered Christianity a Jewish Messianic heresy. In fact, the Jews did not consider Christianity a separate religion from Judaism until the Second Century. We know from history that Nero began an empire wide persecution of Christians after the Great Fire of AD 64, and then he eventually killed the Apostles Peter and Paul in Rome. Some historians estimate that nearly 500,000 Christians were put to death during this time of persecution. Nero was nicknamed "The Beast" by the Roman Senate and there are accounts of Nero dressing as a beast and mauling the bodies of men and women as they were tied to stakes. After the mauling, they were then eventually ignited at night to light Nero's gardens.

c) Notice the souls of the martyrs are under the altar. This is the Altar of Incense. We see a better description of it in Revelation 8. On this Altar there is no sacrifice for sin. Only the sacrifice of worship and prayer to the Lord. Martyrs who die in Christ are lovingly positioned in the place of deepest intimacy with Him.

Revelation 6:10

a) The martyrs intercede for the justice of God to avenge their blood. In Genesis 4:10, we learn blood has a voice. We also know from Leviticus 17:11 that life is in the blood.

b) Only the Lord is the righteous Judge. The judgments of God are perfect and holy, true and right.

Revelation 6:11

a) It was mentioned earlier the Seals, Trumpets and Bowls are the same narrative repeated in increasing intensity and scope of content.

b) The martyrs were told to wait.

c) They were given a white robe to wear. This is the covering of purity, and innocence. First, their faith is pure and true because they did not deny their Savior. Second, loving Christ is no crime because Christian character denies evil and wrong doing. Christianity expresses itself through acts of love, service, supernatural power, and grace.

d) God is slow to anger and full of lovingkindness. We see in Scripture God gives people time and abundant opportunities to come to faith, to experience His love and grace in their lives. Even the Apostle Paul said he tried to destroy the Church of Jesus Christ before his conversion on the road to Damascus.

e) In verse 11, we see that the Lord has a set limit to the number of those who have suffered for His Name. This is an expression of His sovereignty. Jesus pronounced judgment on Jerusalem in Matthew 23:34-35 – "Therefore, behold, I am sending you prophets and wise men and scribes; some of them you will kill and crucify, and some of them you will scourge in your synagogues, and persecute from city to city, so that upon you may fall the guilt of all the righteous blood shed on earth, from the blood of righteous Abel to the blood of Zechariah, the son of Berechiah, whom you murdered between the temple and the altar."

Revelation 6:12

a) Matthew 27:45-54 says that darkness covered the land and an earthquake split rocks and tore the veil of the Temple in two. The darkness showed creation mourning the death of the Son, and the earthquake that ripped the veil in two symbolized Jesus body being the true veil, and through His torn body we all have access to the Father.

Revelation 6:13-14

a) To properly interpret this section - and most of Revelation - we need to interpret it from the position of Hebrew/First Century thought and culture. In prophetic Scripture, we see stars, moon and sun referring to governmental power and ruling authorities. We need to go back to Genesis to find the interpretation of this verse. *(See Genesis 37:9)*

b) Many times in Old Testament Scripture we see the stars, moon, sun, etc., being symbolic of ruling authorities and governmental powers. *(See Joel 2:10, Joel 3:15, Obadiah 1:4)*

c) What we have here is an intense description of the Lord overturning authorities and powers in Jerusalem. The destruction of the Old Covenant Temple needed to fall as it was not useful anymore to mediate between humankind and God, as well as, the judgment of the governmental authorities who condemned Christ and denied Him being Messiah. We have the Old Covenant being put to death by the New Covenant that Jesus cut with His blood.

Revelation 6:15-16

a) Josephus gives an account of the leaders and followers who were fighting the Romans during the siege of Jerusalem leaving the city and hiding in the subterranean caves in the area and hiding from the destruction of the Roman army. It was Josephus' position that Jerusalem was being judged by God for Israel's rebellion, the murder of James the Just and many other men who were considered holy.

b) We see no one was able to stand or hide from the wrath of the Lamb as Jerusalem was judged for her rejection of Messiah.

c) Josephus Book 6, Chapter 9, Section 5 – "by God Himself, and fled immediately to that valley which is under Siloam, where they again recovered themselves out of the dread they were in for a while, and ran violently against that part of the Roman wall which lay on that side; but as their courage was too much depressed to make their attacks with sufficient force, and their power was now broken with fear and affliction, they were repulsed by the guards, and dispersing themselves at distances from each other, went down into the subterranean caverns."

CHAPTER SEVEN

Chapter Seven is an interlude between the Sixth Seal and the opening of the Seventh Seal. In this chapter, we see the loving care of God for His people being expressed as He orchestrates the sealing of His people and a time of peace before the destruction of Jerusalem. It is important to mention the Church of Jerusalem escaped the siege of AD 70 and fled to Pella. Not one Christian is recorded as being killed in the destruction of Jerusalem. Jesus prophesied this in Matthew 24.

One thing we can be sure of is that we can trust the Scriptures and their prophecies. Over and over in Scripture, we see things taking place that were fulfilled in history just as they were predicted by the Scriptures. If we were members of the Seven Churches who received the Revelation, we would be comforted to know the Lord's word is true, reliable, and that He cares and loves His people through the worst of times. The Revelation is the promise of Gods care and deliverance from all trials and tribulations.

As we complete the Interlude of Revelation 7, we find this is one of the most glorious, encouraging and promise filled sections of the Book of Revelation. Imagine yourself as First Century Christian who was enduring the difficulties the Early Church faced. These verses in Revelation 7:9-17 would have imparted hope, courage, faith and perseverance in your walk with Jesus.

Even today we gain the same encouragement that the Early Church received from this section of Scripture called the Interlude. We may even be more encouraged when we learn that the Great Tribulation is over and the contemporary Church of Jesus Christ will not be facing the Destruction of Jerusalem, the persecutions of Nero, Domitian, and others found in the Apostolic Age of the Church.

Revelation 7:1

a) It is important to keep in mind the symbolic nature of the apocalyptic writing style of the Old Testament prophets and the Revelation of John. We see the angelic order participating and facilitating God's decrees and declarations. John is seeing in the Spirit, so we can expect that through this trance state God would reveal vast amounts of understanding in pictures.

b) The wind being held back from the four corners of the earth is figurative language describing a set period of time for the purposes of sealing the first fruits of the Jews who received Jesus as Messiah. This was the time between Pentecost and the Destruction of Jerusalem.

c) Four Winds in the OT – Jeremiah 49:32 & Jeremiah 49:36 – these two example verses introduce us to descriptive language of the four winds as being winds of destruction and judgment from God.

d) Earth – Greek – GE – localized area of a region; ie. the land of Judea

e) Sea –Greek – THALASSA – The Red Sea or the Mediterranean Sea

f) Trees – The Roman Army chopped down all the trees in a 15km circumference surrounding Jerusalem.

Revelation 7:2-3

a) Angel from the east or the place of the rising sun – This angel brings a ministry of peace and a declaration of a specified time on which the first fruits of the Jewish Nation would be saved by believing in Messiah. These angels have the ministry of protecting the Jews who were saved by believing in Messiah. The weeping may last for the night, but joy comes in the morning. From the place of the rising sun or the morning glory come the promises of God. They are new every day.

b) Having a seal on the foreheads remind us of the phylacteries the Covenant people of God wore on their foreheads and arms. *(See Exodus 13:16 & Matthew 23:5)*

c) Being sealed on the forehead – This is the most visible place of the human body and it is the boldest place to have a mark.

d) Servants of our God – Greek – DOULOS – metaphor. One who gives himself up to another's will whose service is used by Christ in extending and advancing his cause among men – devoted to another to the disregard of one's own interests – slave, bondman, man of servile condition – This is the most descriptive language for one who has been completely conquered by the love of Jesus. We can only give ourselves over to the one we trust and know by experience they love us.

Revelation 7:4

a) The 144,000 – these are mentioned in Revelation 14:1-5.

b) The 144,000 is descriptive language for the whole amount of the Jews who believed in Jesus as Messiah during the Apostolic Age of the Early Church. Verse 4 tells us they are Israelites from the 12 tribes. Acts 6:7 tells us a great many priests believed in Jesus and were added to the Church in Jerusalem. Also, more than 3,000 were saved at Pentecost, in addition to these, believers were added daily to the Church in Jerusalem in Acts 2:47. There was a significant amount of Jews who became believers in Jesus and birthed the Church from Jerusalem.

c) The 144,000 are Jews, not Gentiles.

d) 12x12 – 12 is the number of fullness of God's people (12 tribes), or the government of God (12 Apostles). The number 144,000 imply the conversion of many Jewish people. *(See Romans 9-11)*

Revelation 7:5-8

a) This list corresponds to all the Tribes of Israel who were present during the lifetime of Jesus until the destruction of the Temple in AD 70. All the official genealogies were destroyed in the fire that burned the Temple. The only genealogy to survive was that of Jesus.

b) Notice the tribes of Dan and Ephraim are missing. These two tribes were destroyed by their idol worship and apostasy many of hundreds of years before the First Century.

c) The demise of the Tribe of Ephraim – Judges 17 gives an account of a man of Ephraim named Micah, who erected a shrine of an idol, made an ephod and obtained a Levite from Judah to be an illegal priest, and then led Ephraim into idolatry by forsaking the Tabernacle. Over time, Dan fell away from the Covenant and were destroyed in captivity. They reaped the Deuteronomy 28 curses for being Law breakers. Isaiah 7:8 – "For the head of Aram is Damascus, and the head of Damascus is only Rezin. Within sixty-five years Ephraim will be too shattered to be a people."

d) The demise of the Tribe of Dan – In Judges 18, we see the tribe of Dan taking Micah's idols and his priest and continued worshiping the idols until the captivity. Amos 8:14 prophesies their total destruction – "As for those who swear by the guilt of Samaria, Who say, 'As your god lives, O Dan,' And, 'As the way of Beersheba lives,' They will fall and not rise again."

e) It is historically proven that at the time of the First Century, these two tribes were no longer a people who could be recognized as tribes of Israel.

Revelation 7:9

a) The great multitude no one could count – John is seeing the whole collective Church who has overcome the Great Tribulation. We will expound this in more detail when we comment on Revelation 7:14. The Greek basically says this is a crowd of people that is too big to count. This is an expression to describe the whole mass of people who are in view in John's Interlude Vision before the opening of the Seventh Seal. The comment is not literal, but a figure of speech to describe a large crowd.

b) From every nation – Greek – ETHNOS – a people group

c) Tribe – Greek – PHYLE – those descending from the patriarch Jacob – The great multitude includes the Jews who received Jesus as Messiah. This includes the 144,000 mentioned in the beginning of Chapter Seven.

d) People – Greek – LAOS – of the human family, a people group, tribe, etc.

e) Language – Greek – GLOSSA – dialects or languages used particular people groups.

f) It is important to note that by the mid-AD60's the Church had evangelized the known civilized world *(See Colossians 1:6)* It would make sense that all who endured the Great Tribulation would have come from all of people groups of the Roman Empire.

g) Standing before the throne and before the Lamb – This beautiful poetic language describes the position of those who are faithful to God and have overcome the world. To be face to face with the Godhead, and see the Godhead in full glory is an amazing thought. They are standing before the throne and the Lamb described in Revelation 4.

h) White Robes – Greek – STOL – outer garments worn by priests, kings or men of rank. White describes the purity and holiness of those who have been saved, and the outer garment speaks of their position as priests before God. Notice the crowd is not described as gender specific. All who overcome in Jesus Christ are arrayed in white and have a priestly function to minister to the Lord before the throne.

i) Palm Branches – This is a symbol of victory in the ancient world. We see a similar display in Matthew 21 at the Triumphal Entry of Jesus into Jerusalem. John sees the future of those who have received the Revelation, believed the gospel and have stayed true to the Lord despite persecution, martyrdom, hardships and trials. We should not assume all of the multitude had been martyred, but can assume all have overcome the world through Jesus.

Revelation 7:10

a) We see the interrelated working of salvation of the Father and Jesus. John 3:16-17 – "For God so loved the world, that He gave His only begotten Son, that whoever believes in Him shall not perish, but have eternal life. "For God did not send the Son into the world to judge the world, but that the world might be saved through Him."

Revelation 7:11-12

a) Revelation 5:11 is in view here. Verse 11 describes the glorious angelic assemblies of God, who worship and adore the Living God. The angelic realm is awed by the salvation that was given to mankind through the cross. 1 Peter 1:12 – "It was revealed to them that they were not serving themselves, but you, in these things which now have been announced to you through those who preached the gospel to you by the Holy Spirit sent from heaven — things into which angels long to look."

b) In verse 12, we see the Sevenfold DOXA (glory) of worship offered to the Lord. We see this same Sevenfold DOXA in Revelation 5. Seven is the number of completeness. The fullness of the expressions of worship contains these seven concepts: Praise, Glory, Wisdom, Thanks, Honor, Power and Strength.

c) The Amen is the expression of the strongest agreement from the angelic order. It is interesting to note that even angels have emotions and are capable of the deep expression of their hearts in worship toward God.

Revelation 7:13-14

a) The Great Tribulation – Matthew 24:21-22 – "For then there will be a great tribulation, such as has not occurred since the beginning of the world until now, nor ever will. Unless those days had been cut short, no life would have been saved; but for the sake of the elect those days will be cut short." – MEGAS THLIPSIS – the large pressing – is used in both Revelation 7 and Matthew 24:21. The Great Tribulation of the Church began with the Jewish persecution of the Church in Jerusalem, to the destruction of Jerusalem in AD 70, and continued through the great persecutions of Nero, etc. The good news is that the Great Tribulation ended in the era of the Early Church, and will never happen again.

b In Verse 14, we see the beautiful poetic language of the blood of Jesus making our robes/coverings white. This speaks the purity of the blood of Jesus. *(See 1 Peter 1:18-19)*

Revelation 7:15-17

a) Before the throne to serve day and night – This is everlasting priestly presence, and throne room experiential worship. This is unbroken fellowship. Many commentators include the whole Church in these promises as we see a parallel section found in Revelation 19:7-8.

b) Spread His tent over them – Psalm 91 promises in fullness are in view here. The Lord is our covering, our shield and loving protector for eternity.

c) Never hunger or thirst – There is no bodily suffering in heaven, or spiritual lack in heaven. How much more should we pray "on earth as it is in heaven!"

d) Jesus our Shepherd – Greek – POIMAIN – to feed, to tend a flock, keep sheep, to rule, govern, to nourish, to cherish one's body, to serve the body, to supply the requisites for the soul's need

e) Guide us to springs of living water – Jesus fulfills His promise in John 4:13-14 – Jesus is the sufficiency for all who love Him.

f) God (Father) will wipe away all tears – This is metaphor for the caring healing touch from our Father in heaven.

CHAPTER EIGHT

Revelation Chapter Eight begins the Second cycle of Sevens. As I mentioned earlier in this commentary, the book of Revelation is a cyclical book that tells and re-tells the same account of salvation history, but in varying degrees of intensity and scope.

The first set of Sevens were concluded with the completion of Chapter Seven. In Chapter Eight, we begin the re-telling of the same story of the first Seven Seals, as the Seventh Seal opens the cycle for the Seven Trumpets. The Seven Trumpet cycle is told from the perspective of the spirit realm and the spiritual warfare which accompanies the destruction of Jerusalem and whole of salvation history.

Before we move on, it would be helpful to review the First cycle of the Seven Seals. The rider on the white horse is Jesus Christ who is portrayed as the victorious conquering King. The rider on the red horse is the Roman Army being led by Vespasian and Titus. The rider on the black horse was the famine that accompanied the siege of Jerusalem. The fifth seal brought into view those who were martyred for Christ during the Jewish and Roman persecutions of the First Century, and their intercession for justice. The sixth seal brought into view the signs of God's coming judgment to Jerusalem for rejecting the Messiah Jesus Christ. Then the Interlude brings into view the encouraging vision of those who stayed faithful to the Lord, of both Jews and Gentiles through the great tribulation of the destruction of Jerusalem and the Jewish/Roman persecutions of the Early Church.

The book of Revelation is 3 cycles of seven, representing the 777 complete view of salvation history from the birth of the Church to the Second Coming of Jesus Christ.

It is important for us to mention the theological concept of hermeneutics as we continue in this chapter. A hermeneutic is the preexisting bias, prejudice, or world view that we as individuals use to color our interpretations of Scripture. Our hermeneutic drives us to conclusions and interpretations of the Bible which shape our views of the nature and character of God, salvation, healing, spiritual gifts, eschatology, the Covenants, and many other important theological positions that ultimately affect even our most simple expressions of the Christian faith.

The hermeneutic I am using in this commentary of Revelation is the Partial Preterist perspective, with a Post-Millennial view of the future of salvation history. It is the position that basically believes most of the Book of Revelation was written to the First Century Church, just before the destruction of Jerusalem, and most of the Revelation was fulfilled in that time. The bulk of the book of Revelation has been fulfilled with exception of the physical return of Jesus Christ, the resurrection of the dead, and the Great White Throne Judgment. This approach to the Book of Revelation sees the future of the world in very positive light because the Old Covenant was put away by the destruction of Jerusalem in AD70, and the New Covenant was confirmed by the destruction of the Temple, thereby confirming the Apostles preaching of Jesus as Messiah. This approach continues its positive view of the future of the world and the Church because the Judgments of God were directed at the apostate Land of Judea, the Roman Empire and the people that rejected Jesus as Messiah in the First Century. This does not take away from the Judgment of God to come on those who reject Him and His offer of salvation today. Lastly, this view is very positive because it sees the future of world in terms of the mercy of God in the New Covenant, and the Church's ability to convert the vast number of people in the world through preaching of the goodness of God, and our ability to bring reformation to all realms of society. It is important to mention that this view was the prominent view of the Church until the early 1900's.

As we learned in previous pages, the three cycles of seven found in the Seals, Trumpets, and Bowls are basically the same narrative told from increasingly intense perspectives, and are in relation to the destruction of Jerusalem, the Temple, and the Roman Empire's ability to persecute Christians. Chapter Eight is from the perspective of the Angelic/Spiritual Realm.

Revelation 8:1

a) The silence in heaven is a significant contrast when compared to the glorious DOXA of Chapter Seven.

b) This is something we should pay attention to, as it speaks of two things as the Lamb opens the Seventh Seal: The first being the awesome reverence of God in the angelic realm. There are many times in Scripture where being in the presence of God demands silence. *(See Ecclesiastes 5:2, Job 40:4-5, Psalm 46:10)* The second is an angelic realm in awe of God's judgments and the scope and power of His decrees. No words can describe the awesome power of what has been decreed by God in terms of the finality of them.

Revelation 8:2

a) The symbolism of 7 is found throughout the book of Revelation as it is the divine number of completeness, and finality.

b) Trumpets in Scripture are used for three main purposes: 1) To sound the alarm of war; 2) to gather the assembly to worship or feast; 3) a command to march. In the context of this prophetic book, the Seven Trumpets are the alarm of war against those who have rejected Jesus as Messiah.

c) The seven angels were ones who stood before God in addition to the four living creatures and the 24 elders. The description of their position as being before God tells us something about their status and mission. Being before the Living God tells us that these seven angels were close to the counsels of God in throne room and that these angels were set apart for carrying out the decrees of the Godhead.

d) It is important to mention that we see the pattern of Seven Trumpets in the destruction of Jericho. *(See Joshua 4:8)* This is a prophetic picture of the destruction of those who oppose God and His people. In this account, also note the three cycles of seven symbolizing the totality of God's judgments.

Revelation 8:3-4

a) In Verses 3-5, we see the power of prayer and intercession. In verse 3, we see the altar of incense in the True Temple in heaven. We see similar scene mentioned in Revelation 5:8. A golden censer was only used on the Day of Atonement. The smoke from the censer came from the sacred fire that never burned out on the altar of incense. Hebrews 9 connects this with the Holy of Holies and our access to the true Holy of Holies through Jesus Christ who is our True High Priest in Order of Melchizedek. *(See Numbers 4:14 & Leviticus 16:12)*

b) Our prayers are incense before God and are pleasing to Him. This verse shows that even the angelic realm partners with our prayers. Prayer is described in Revelation as powerful, pleasing to God and full of ability to accomplish what is being prayed for.

c) Acts 10 gives the account of the prayers of Cornelius being an offering before God that released salvation to the Gentiles.

Revelation 8:5

a) The act of the angel hurling the censer to the earth (GE), describes the awesome power and the force of our prayers.

b) Keep in mind the destruction of the land is in view in the Seven Trumpet Judgments. The land mentioned is the Land of Judea, and specifically the Jerusalem and the Temple. The Old Covenant revolved around the Promised Land. As Jesus was rejected by the political and religious rulers of Judea, and as Jesus instituted a New Covenant, the land was worthy of Seven Trumpet Judgments.

c) Peals of thunder, rumblings, flashes of lightings and an earthquake – Symbolism speaking of the unspeakable power of God's throne, His judgments and the majesty of His person. We see a similar manifestation in Revelation 4 in the description of the spiritual atmosphere around His throne.

Revelation 8:6

a) As seen from verse 2, trumpets in Scripture are used for three main purposes: To sound the alarm of war, to gather the assembly to worship or feast, or as a command to march. In the context of this prophetic book, the Seven Trumpets are the alarm of war against those who have rejected Jesus as Messiah.

b) As seen from verse 2, these seven angels were the ones who stood before God in addition to the four living creatures and the 24 elders. The description of their position as being before God tells us something about their status and mission. Being before the Living God tells us that these seven angels were close to the counsels of God in the throne room. These angels were set apart for carrying out the decrees of the Godhead.

Revelation 8:7

a) Verse 7 begins to show us what the angelic spiritual realm looks like when the decrees of the Lamb are carried out by the angels and what their assignments look like in terms of their missions. The Book of Revelation gives us an amazing amount of insight in terms of what the spiritual realm is like. No other book of the Bible gives us this much detail and insight about angels, their assignments and their missions.

b) We see a parallel between the judgments of the Lord on Egypt, and the judgments of the Lamb on the land that rejected Him. To add to this parallel, Egypt oppressed the people of God, and so did the unbelieving Jews who persecuted the Jews who believed Jesus was Messiah. The Book of Acts gives us many detailed accounts of the Jewish persecutions of believers.

c) The NIV and other translations here use the word *earth.* The more proper translation should be *land*, as the Greek word here for earth is GE – GE – country, land enclosed within fixed boundaries, a tract of land, territory, or region.

d) A literal interpretation is not possible here as we see plainly in the text John is in the Spirit, and he is observing angels who exist in the spiritual unseen realm doing things in the spiritual realm that affect the natural realm. The symbolism of hail, blood and fire, are used throughout the OT as descriptions of God's judgments on those who are in rebellion to Him. *(See Genesis 19:24, Exodus 9:18, Exodus 4:9, Psalm 58:10, Isaiah 34:6 & Joel 2:30-31)*

e) The First Trumpet Judgment was directed at the land itself, damaging it and making it unfruitful in its ability to bless people with provision. Josephus gives us detailed accounts of how the Roman Army leveled the land and cut down all the trees, "For all the trees around the city had been cut down for a distance of 90 stadia (10mi/16km)." Again, Josephus wrote, "And truly, the very view itself was a melancholy thing; for those places which were adorned with trees and pleasant gardens, were now become desolate country every way, and its trees were all cut down. Nor could any foreigner that had formerly seen Judea and the most beautiful suburbs of the city, and now saw it as a desert, but lament and mourn sadly at so great a change. For the war had laid all signs of beauty quite waste."

f) Isaiah 40:6-8 – "A voice says, "Call out." Then he answered, "What shall I call out?" All flesh is grass, and all its loveliness is like the flower of the field. The grass withers, the flower fades, When the breath of the LORD blows upon it; Surely the people are grass. The grass withers, the flower fades, but the word of our God stands forever." – These verses in Isaiah add to the symbolic meaning of verse 7, as it uses grass/flowers as a metaphor to contrast the Everlasting Life of God to our mortal lives.

Revelation 8:8-9

a) As the angel blows the Second Trumpet Judgment, we see a huge mountain thrown into the sea. It is important to interpret these two symbols properly to understand the text in the context of its hearers.

b) Mountain – In Scripture, a mountain is symbolic of nations, governments, and authority. Jeremiah 51:25,42, Exodus 15:17, Deuteronomy 33:19, Psalm 30:7 – Jerusalem is described as a mountain. *(See Psalm 48:1, Isaiah 2:3, Isaiah 11:9, Isaiah 27:13)*

c) Sea – In Scripture, a sea is used to speak of a mass of people – Psalm 98:7, Jeremiah 51:36, Jeremiah 51:42, Hosea 1:10, Habakkuk 3:15, Isaiah 57:20, Revelation 13:1

d) In Matthew 21:18-22, Jesus curses the fig tree and tells His disciples they can cast a mountain into the sea by prayer. This is right after His triumphal entry and His battles with the religious leadership of Jerusalem, where He prophesied their destruction for rejecting Him. The fig tree is Jerusalem and the mountain is the Temple. Charles Taylor comments, "There were three parts of the temple: the outer area where the people gathered, the central section where the animals were sacrificed, and the inner part which was the Holy of Holies. When the Roman Army had fought and gained ground to the innermost part, this was the point to which the people inside had retreated. Here, utter destruction took place and the people in this third part died. Not only did the people die, but the Holy of Holies was burned with fire. By this destruction, those who had made their livelihood by supplying the costly furnishings of the temple (much of this being brought in by ships) no longer had any occupation as far as this place was concerned." Let us go to Scripture for the definition of the term *ships:* Revelation 18:19 – And they cast dust on their heads, and cried, weeping and wailing, saying, Alas, alas, that great city, wherein were made rich all that had ships in the sea by reason of her costliness! For in one hour is she made desolate."

e) The mountain thrown into the sea represents the destruction of Jerusalem by Gentiles (Romans). The Second Trumpet is a judgment on the Temple and the economy that came with it.

Revelation 8:10-11

a) The Third Trumpet Judgment shows us a star, who is an angel, named *Wormwood.* The assignment of this angel is to strike the water supply of Jerusalem. This also parallels Isaiah's prophecy of the judgment and fall of Babylon. *(See Isaiah 14:12-15)*

b) Wormwood in Scripture is used to describe the punishment of rebellious Israel. *(See Deuteronomy 29:18, Jeremiah 9:15, Jeremiah 23:15, Lamentations 3:15)* We see a parallel between these verses and the Nile being made bitter by the rotting fish from the judgment of the Lord.

c) Jerusalem had an abundant water supply, as described in 2 Chronicles 32 & 2 Kings 20. Josephus gives us a detailed account of the suffering of the famine in Jerusalem during the siege, resulting in death and disease which polluted the water supply to point where it is was no longer potable.

d) The Third Trumpet Judgment is a judgment on the water supply of Jerusalem. John is making the point that Israel is apostate. She will be judged and destroyed like Egypt and Babylon.

Revelation 8:12

a) The symbolism of the sun, moon, and stars speak of the governmental powers and authorities of Israel. The first mention of the sun, moon and stars being heads of the people is found in Joseph's dream in Genesis 37:9-11. We can see from this perspective that heavenly bodies are used as metaphors for ruling authorities. Stars are also found in Scripture as symbols of angels and demons. *(See Revelation 8:10, Job 38:7, Isaiah 14:13, Daniel 8:10, Jude 1:13)*

b) When the light of Christ is removed from rulers, there is no revelation, and darkness prevails in the hearts of men. The Sanhedrin and the Temple Priests rejected Jesus as Messiah. Jesus is the Light, yet they chose darkness instead.

c) The Fourth Trumpet Judgment is a judgment on the political and religious rulers of Israel.

Revelation 8:13

a) Verse 13 is a transitory verse that highlights the severity of the spiritual realm in terms of God's judgment on the land of Israel that is to come in Chapter Nine. The trumpet blasts to come are even more graphic and intense.

b) It is interesting to note this angel is in the form of an eagle. Another indication that we are dealing with a spiritual reality and not a literal one. Even though there are dimensions of these judgments that manifest in the natural realm, we are seeing the reality of the spiritual realm in this section of the Book of Revelation.

c) As terrible as the judgment of the Godhead on rebellious Israel for rejecting Jesus as Messiah was, God's judgments are always for redemptive purposes. Revelation 9:20-21 tells us the intentions of the Trumpet Judgments are for the opportunity to repent and turn from sin to God.

d) After the destruction of the Jerusalem and Temple, the judgments of God are ceased until the Second Coming of Jesus

Christ. The judgment of the cross satisfies the Father's demand for justice in this Age of Grace.

CHAPTER NINE

Revelation Chapter Nine continues the Seven Trumpet cycle in the context of spiritual warfare in the unseen realms in relation to the destruction of the land of Judea, Jerusalem and the Temple.

The approach to the interpretation of Chapter Nine is from the Partial Preterist perspective in order to show us the historical context of the book of Revelation as it was written to the Seven Churches in the First Century to encourage them to stay true to the gospel and to overcome the persecutions they faced from the Jews and the Romans.

The Book of Revelation is relevant to us today because it teaches us the authority of Jesus Christ as King, His divinity, the authority of the Church of Jesus Christ, the description of spirit realm, angels, the defeat of Satan and demons, and the hope of the Second Coming of Jesus and the eternal order that is to come. It is important that we understand the Book of Revelation from the context of the First Century, as it keeps us from projecting this book onto our culture and coloring how we view the future.

The Seven Trumpet cycle continues in the context of spiritual warfare in the unseen realms in relation to the destruction of the land of Judea, Jerusalem and the Temple.

The Sixth Trumpet is about to blow, and we will see the most descriptive language on the subject of spiritual warfare and the assignment of demons ever found in Scripture. As we continue to read through the Revelation, I want to remind us that we are approaching the Revelation from the Partial Preterist View which sees a partial fulfillment of the Revelation in the First Century, and in the real history surrounding the destruction of Judea, Jerusalem and the Temple.

The point of this verse by verse commentary of the Revelation, is to demystify the book. We need to place it in the proper context of the First Century hearer to prove the prophecies of Jesus concerning the generation who rejected Him, His prophecies of the destruction of Jerusalem, the Temple, and the desolation of the land were actually fulfilled in the First Century. To project the Book of Revelation into the future is to dismiss the real history of Jews, the Church, and the prophecies of Jesus, thus engaging in very serious speculations about the future we live in now.

Revelation 9:1

a) The fifth angel blows his trumpet and the forces of demonic hoards are released on the land (GE).

b) The star fallen from heaven/sky – The Greek word for heaven – OURANOS – the region above the sidereal heavens, the seat of order of things eternal and consummately perfect where God dwells and other heavenly beings – This fallen star is Satan. Luke 10:18 – And He said to them, "I was watching Satan fall from heaven like lightning. "Behold, I have given you authority to tread on serpents and scorpions, and over all the power of the enemy, and nothing will injure you." We see many times in Scripture where a star is used in the context of spiritual beings, as mentioned in previous chapters.

c) The key to the Abyss – Greek – KLEIS – the keeper of the keys has the power to open and to shut – metaph. In the NT, to denote power and authority of various kinds.

d) The Abyss in Scripture is a descriptive word for the place that is farthest extreme from the dwelling place of God. Jonah 2:2-6 & Luke 8:31 describe the Abyss as the prison of demons. Romans 10:7 describes the Abyss as the realm of the dead.

e) To summarize verse 1, we see the fallen star/Satan was given authority to bring torment on the land for their rejection Jesus as Messiah. When Jesus was present in the land, the land of Judea was blessed by the benefits of His ministry and teaching. *(Read Matthew 12:43-45)*

Revelation 9:2

a) The smoke darkening the sun and the sky speak of the spiritual description of not having the light of Life, but being darkened by the darkness which accompanies the demonic realm. We learned in previous chapters that the sun, stars, and moon are metaphors for rulers, authorities, and powers. *(See Genesis 37:9)*

Revelation 9:3-6

a) Verses 3-6 give us the description and mission of these demons who bring affliction to the people of the land. These woes are worse because they are focused on people who are made in God's image.

b) The Lord Jesus commands protection for His own, as those who are sealed by the Holy Spirit are exempted from tormenting demonic attacks. It is important to mention again that not one Christian was killed in the destruction of Jerusalem. Also, the Book of Acts shows us Christians may have been persecuted and mocked, but no Christians are tormented and afflicted by demons. We can be assured that though we are challenged by the demonic realm, we are not possessed by them, and the demonic realm does not have the authority to torture a Christian. The level of demonic influence in a Christian's life is determined by his or her level of agreement with darkness.

c) 5 months – The season of locust invasions in the land of Judea were typically from May to September. Joel uses locusts as a symbolic description of invading armies that will bring destruction to Jerusalem. We also see locust plagues on Egypt as a sign of God's judgment. In this case, we see demonic locusts bring spiritual torment to those who have clung to the Old Covenant, rejecting the New Covenant. It is interesting to note here that Titus focused his attack on Jerusalem starting May 1, AD70 and on September 27, AD70, Titus commanded the city with absolute control. The historical account plainly shows the effects of the demonic spirits associated with rebellion, war, immorality and murder.

d) Josephus is quoted with describing the level of demonic influence in the city of Jerusalem during the siege, "With their insatiable hunger for loot, they ransacked the houses of the wealthy, murdered men and violated women for sport; they drank their spoils with blood, and from mere satiety they shamelessly gave themselves up to effeminate practices, plaiting their hair and putting on women's clothes, drenching themselves with perfumes and painting their eyelids to make themselves attractive. They copied not merely the dress, but also the passions of women, devising in their excess of licentiousness unlawful pleasures in which they wallowed as in a brothel. Thus, they entirely polluted the city with their foul practices. Yet though they wore women's faces, their hands were murderous. They would approach with mincing steps, then suddenly become fighting men, and, whipping out their swords from under their dyed cloaks, they would run through every passerby." Josephus describes other types of demonically inspired drama in Jerusalem – loss of the ability to reason by rulers and rebel leaders, attacking gangs, roving mobs, cannibalism, robberies, wild and unrealistic claims of false prophets, mass murders, executions and suicides.

Revelation 9:7-10

a) Verses 7-10 re-tells the scene in verses 1-6 in greater detail and repeats the narrative for clarity and effect.

b) Horses – war, power in battle, symbol of power in the ancient world.

c) Something like crowns of gold – "like" – false authority – real crowns of gold are reserved for God's those who love and serve God.

d) Human faces – these demons reflect the fallen nature of man without God.

e) Women's hair – false covering and beauty, and false glory

f) Lion's teeth – the power to tear, false wisdom, and lying

g) Breastplates of iron, wings and thundering sounds describe their number and their assignment to war against humanity.

h) Scorpion stings tingle, burn, can cause swelling in the tongue, affect eye sight, but are almost never mortal. Scorpion stings are unbearably uncomfortable.

i) The mission of the demonic realm is to cause torment, loss of peace, discomfort, and fear to the souls and bodies of people. The five months is repeated for clarity. Any First Century Jewish believer would have been familiar with the symbolism of the section of Scripture and would understand the locust reference to this demonic attack being released as a sign of God's judgment on those who rejected Jesus as Messiah, by invading armies of demons that not only inspire the leadership of Jerusalem, but the Roman Legions invading Judea and sieging the city.

Revelation 9:11

a) Satan is identified in verse 11 as the leader of the demonic realm. It is important for us to note that he is a created being, not omnipresent, not self-existent, or omniscient. Christians should never error and equate Satan with these types of qualities which distinctly belong to the Godhead. *(See Colossians 1:15-20)*

Revelation 9:12

a) The next two woes are increasingly destructive and horrible to those who deny the Lordship of Jesus Christ. The first woe did not include death; the next woe is the spiritual description of war and horrors which accompany it.

Revelation 9:13

a) The sixth angel blows the trumpet – We have learned that in Scripture trumpets were used to sound the alarm of war; to gather the assembly to worship or feast; or as a command to march. In the context of this prophetic book, the Seven Trumpets are the alarm of war against those who have rejected Jesus as Messiah.

b) The voice coming from the horns of the golden altar that is before God. The symbolism is important to note here: This is the true altar before God's throne. The horns of the altar are significant because this was the place where the sins of the community were covered by blood in the Old Covenant Sacrificial System. *(See Leviticus 4:13-18)* A First Century believer would have connected this altar to the earthly altar in Jerusalem and would have seen its fulfillment in Jesus Christ's sacrifice for sin. The symbolism of gold represents the Royal Authority of God, and the abundance of His power and the wealth of His Kingdom.

c) The voice from the altar that is before God's throne is authoritative and holds the power of the decree of God. God's people are covered by the blood of Jesus have access to His presence and throne.

Revelation 9:14-15

a) The Great River Euphrates is the Northern most natural boundary between the land of Judea and the pagan kingdoms of the North, i.e. Babylonians, Assyrians, etc. In Scripture, the area of the Euphrates is described as the place where the judgments of God on the land of Israel originate. *(See Jer. 6:1, 22; 10:22; 13:20; 25:9, 26; 46:20, 24; 47:2; Ezek. 26:7; 38:6, 15; 39:2)*

b) A First Century Jewish believer would have associated the area as the place where the judgments of God come on the land of Israel.

c) The reference to the angels being bound – Greek – DE – to bind – bound with chains – to bind, fasten with chains, to throw into chains – or can be used as a metaphor for satanic influence – the same word is used in Luke 13:16 by Jesus to describe the woman who was bent over by satanic influence in her life. These four angels can be identified as angels who are in allegiance with Satan. *(See Revelation 9:11)*

d) Their assignment is to release the hell of war and death on the land in response the Jewish rejection of Jesus.

e) It is important to note that their assignment was at a specific time, day, month and year. If this already happened in history, we would have no expectation of anything like this in the future.

f) To kill a third of mankind – The Greek word ANTHROPOS is used here in verse 15 and it simply means people, male or female. When we think of the word in our cultural context, we think of the whole human race. This is not in view here. It refers to a large group of people. History tells us vast numbers of people perished in the destruction of the land of Judea and during the siege of Jerusalem. Josephus says approximately 1.1 million died in Jerusalem alone.

Revelation 9:16

a) The number of the mounted troops – 200 million – Greek – DISMYRIAS – double myriad, an innumerable number – To take this number literally is to miss the point of what is being described. A vast demonic army will be loosed on the land,

Jerusalem and the Temple. The identity of these mounted troops will be given to us verses 17-19. It is also error to associate this demon army with a physical army, as the clear context of these verses in the taking place "in the Spirit".

Revelation 9:17-18

a) The symbolism of the demon horses and riders.

b) Fiery Red – A description of demonic anger and the association with the Dragon/Satan.

c) Dark Blue – As opposed to the heavenly blue hues of God's realm, speaks of them belonging to a false dominion.

d) Yellow like sulfur – This is symbolic of being allied with hell as sulfur and brimstone come from hell.

e) Horses with lions' heads – Symbolic for the fierceness and devouring attacks that these demons loose upon the land. Horses are symbols of warfare, and power in warfare in Scripture.

f) Out of mouth – No words, only the stench of hell. There is no breath of life in the mouths of Satan or demons. The absence of the Breath of Life brings death.

Revelation 9:19

a) The power was in their mouths and tails – Again, we continue with the symbolic description of the demon horses. The tails like snakes, continue the symbolism of these demon horses being empowered by the serpent, Satan.

b) The Greek word for injury used here is interesting. ADIKE – to act unjustly or wickedly, to sin, to be a criminal, to have violated the laws in some way, to do wrong, to hurt. We can see from a natural reading of the original use of the word that this would be injurious in terms of sin that hurts the souls of people and brings spiritual death, as well as, physical death when it is manifested in the natural realm.

c) We are seeing a very descriptive narrative of the spiritual warfare that accompanied God's judgment on Jerusalem, as this was the generation who rejected Jesus Christ as Messiah. Many times, in Old Testament Scripture, we see God using the enemies of Israel to be tools of judgment, and then in turn we see God judge their enemies according to what they had done to Israel. We see this same flow in Revelation as Satan and his demons are judged and are destroyed in the lake of fire. *(See Revelation 20)*

Revelation 9:20

a) The Old Covenant Temple and worship system became devoid of life when Jesus was sacrificed for sin on the cross, was raised from the dead, and ascended into heaven. The Temple worship had become useless and the symbolic Temple elements that were to lead Israel to Jesus became idolatrous.

b) Gold, silver, bronze, stone and wood were all used in Temple worship as either building materials, or materials associated with the Temple instruments.

c) When God is not present, every expression of worship is void and open to the influence of demons. The Temple and the Law at this point had become useless and lacked any ability to save, cover sin, or please God.

d) John refers to Psalm 115 in Verse 20.

e) Josephus gives a detailed list of supernatural documented warnings given to this generation to cause them to repent, as listed in the following pages:

1. Sign of the Son of Man in the sky – Josephus documented seven signs in detail. The parallel passage here is Luke 21:11. "Fearful sights and great signs from heaven."

2. A meteor in the shape of a sword hung over Jerusalem for 12 months of which he eye-witnessed.

3. On the eighth month of Zanthicus, before the feast of unleavened bread, a light shone around the altar as bright as the light of day for about ½ hour.

4. At the last Passover before the destruction of Jerusalem, a heifer [female cow] gave birth to a lamb [newborn sheep] on its way to the sacrificial altar. Josephus documents this in detail. This is the same season in which our Lord became the One sacrifice.

5. In the night, a bronze gate to the Temple which required the strength of 20 men to close was blown wide open.

6. After a Passover feast, before the setting of the sun, chariots and armed men were seen in the air, passing around Jerusalem.

7. At Pentecost that same year, the priests in the Temple heard murmuring that eventually became loud voices which said, "Let us depart from here."

8. Josephus says the most fearful sign was a

> prophet from the lower class named Ananus, who during the feast of tabernacles before the destruction of Jerusalem, declared all throughout the city, "A voice from the east, a voice from the west, a voice from the four winds, a voice against Jerusalem, a voice against bridegrooms and brides, a voice against the whole people." This man was scourged, but showed no sign of fear or pain, he prophesied this over and over, and became the first casualty in the siege from a Roman war engine, as he prophesied his own death.

Revelation 9:21

a) God's judgments on Jerusalem were for the purpose of repentance. The Lord gives every opportunity for the human heart to repent. Greek – METANOE – to change one's mind, i.e. to repent, to change one's mind for better, heartily to amend with abhorrence of one's past sins.

b) John lists the crimes of the generation of those who rejected Jesus.

c) Murders – The crucifixion of Jesus, the stoning of Steven, and the Church. *(See Acts 2:23, 36; 3:14-15; 4:26; 7:51-52, 58-60)*

d) Sorceries/Magic Arts – Simon the Sorcerer *(See Acts 8:9, 11; 13:6-11; 19:13-15; cf. Rev. 18:23; 21:8; 22:15)*

e) Sexual Immoralities – The description of sexual sins, rape, and spiritual adultery were all present in this generation. *(See Rev 2:14; 2:20; 2:21; 9:21; 14:8; 17:2 [twice]; 17:4; 18:3 [twice]; 18:9; 19:2)* – Josephus comments, "These men, therefore, trampled upon all the laws of man, and laughed at the laws of God; and as for the oracles of the prophets, they ridiculed them as the tricks of jugglers; yet did these prophets foretell many things concerning the rewards of virtue, and punishments of vice, which when these zealots violated, they occasioned the fulfilling of those very prophecies belonging to their own country." – "Neither did any other city ever suffer such miseries, nor did any age ever breed a generation more fruitful in wickedness than this was, from the beginning of the world." – "I suppose that had the Romans made any longer delay in coming against these villains, the city would either have been swallowed up by the ground opening upon them, or been overflowed by water, or else been destroyed by such thunder as the country of Sodom perished by, for it had brought forth a generation of men much more atheistical than were those that suffered such punishments; for by their madness it was that all the people came to be destroyed."

f) Thefts – This crime in the OT is associated with apostasy. *(See Isa. 61:8; Jer. 7:9-10; Ezek. 22:29; Hos. 4:1-2; Mark 11:17; Rom. 2:21; James 5:1)*

CHAPTER TEN

Revelation Chapter Ten is part of a second brief interlude. This interlude comes between the blowing of the Sixth and Seventh trumpets. It includes the Mighty Angel and the Mystery of God that is becoming accomplished and John eating the Little Scroll. This interlude continues into Chapter Eleven with the Testimony of the Two Witnesses.

This second interlude is consistent with the flow of Revelation as we have seen in the previous interlude of Chapter Seven. Revelation Chapter Ten is an encouragement to the Church that displays a wide panoramic view of the power of the Gospel, and John's eating of the Little Scroll which empowers his prophetic assignment.

Revelation 10:1

a) Many commentators have identified this angel as Jesus because of the description of the angel. I do not see that in this text for two reasons: 1) Jesus is never described as an angel in the New Testament or in Revelation. He is described as the Lamb and the Lion; 2) This Mighty Angel swears by God Himself. Jesus, being a Person of the Godhead, would not swear to Himself.

b) The description of the Mighty Angel is described in great glory, size and power. The symbolism describing him tells us something about the authority and assignment of this angel.

c) Mighty Angel – Greek – Mighty/Strong – ISCHYROS – strong either in body or in mind, of one who has strength of soul to sustain the attacks of Satan, strong and therefore exhibiting many excellences – This angel was created by God with mighty power to announce the fulfillment of the purpose of the gospel.

d) Robed in a cloud – This angel is clothed with the glory of God. A cloud is referenced to the glory of God in Exodus 19:16; 40:35, Numbers 9:19, Deuteronomy 5:22, 2 Chronicles 5:13.

e) Rainbow above his head – The rainbow speaks of God's covenant promises. The angel as a supernatural rainbow/ headdress that identifies him as one who has some type of ministry that concerns the Covenants of God. This angel does announce the fulfillment of the mystery of God, which is what Paul describes as the revealing of the Gospel. There will be more to come on this subject when we get to verse 7.

f) Face like the sun – This angel is reflecting the effects of having been basking in the presence of the Godhead. Just as Moses' face displayed the radiant glory of God, this angel carries this same manifestation, but only in greater intensity. *(See Exodus 34:35)*

g) Legs like fiery pillars – The proper word would be feet – Greek – POUS – Often in ancient, thought the foot is referenced as being placed on top of the vanquished when this word is used. *(See Strong's G4228)* This angel is an angel of victory.

Revelation 10:2-3

a) The angel held a little scroll which is a scroll of prophecy to empower John to continue his prophetic ministry. This is another reason to believe this angel is not Jesus. This angel carries a little scroll; Jesus possesses *The Scroll.*

b) The angel's foot is on the land and the sea. Greek – GE for land

and THALASSA for sea. This references a localized region of the land and the Mediterranean Sea or Red Sea, not the global earth land mass or the totality of the oceans. Having his feet on the sea and land speak of God's victory over the land of Judea, and the sea surrounding that area. That region may have rejected and crucified Messiah, but the eternal Gospel will be victorious over those who rejected Jesus.

c) Roar of a lion – This is symbolic language for the ferocity of the angels' message and the kingly authority that backed his voice. Lions were the symbol of kingly power and authority in the ancient world, as the lion is a fierce predator and has no natural enemy.

d) Voice of the Seven Thunders – George Eldon Ladd in his commentary states the Greek use of the definite article in the phrase "seven thunders" indicates that something is known or familiar to the hearers. Whatever the seven thunders are, we cannot be dogmatic in saying, but I suggest the seven thunders are the authoritative voice of a decree from God. It would seem to me that the Christians who received the Revelation, as well as Christians today, would recognize God's voice that sounds like seven thunders.

Revelation 10:4

a) Whatever the seven thunders spoke, we are not privileged to know. The Apostle Paul describes his third heaven experience in 2 Corinthians 12, telling he heard inexpressible things that man is not permitted to tell. Some revelatory experiences with God are so sweet they should not be told. It is proper to keep the secret of Lord sometimes. All lovers have sweet secrets between each other.

Revelation 10:5-7

a) As the angel swears by the Creator God, he declares that when the Seventh angel blows his trumpet the mystery of God will be accomplished. We have mentioned before that Revelation is a cyclical, repetitive prophecy which gives us the same narrative over and over in different perspectives and intensifying degrees.

b) The Mystery of God – It is always best practice to use Scripture to interpret Scripture. The Mystery of God is not a mystery as we understand it in modern terms. Mystery - Greek - MYSTERION - something hidden, hidden purpose or will - In Romans 11:25, Romans 16:25, 1 Corinthians 2:7, Ephesians 3:3,4,9, Colossians 1:26, Colossians 2:2, Colossians 4:3 all describe the Mystery of God as being the Gospel: Jesus Christ's crucifixion/ sacrifice for sin, resurrection, ascension, and Second Coming. The New Testament explains the Mystery of God in the Person of Jesus Christ, the prophecies of the Old Testament in terms of Christ's first coming, sin sacrifice, power, Second Coming the glory of the Church, and the Eternal Kingdom.

c) If we reference the blowing of the Seventh Trumpet in Revelation 11:18, we see the Mystery of God accomplished by the establishment of the eternal order. The Seventh Trumpet has not been blown yet, we are still waiting for that one to blow. This trumpet is mentioned in 1 Thessalonians 4:16.

Revelation 10:8

a) It is interesting to note that this mighty angel suddenly became small enough for John to take the little scroll out of his hand. This highlights how changing and fluid the apocalyptic writings of the Bible are. It is error to interpret Scripture from strict literal interpretations. It is more reliable to interpret Scripture in terms of symbolism, culture, history, and first mentions in Scripture.

Revelation 10:9-11

a) We see a similar encounter in Ezekiel 3, when the Lord commanded Ezekiel to eat a scroll that would empower him to speak the words of God.

b) John's scroll is sweet like honey in his mouth, but sours his stomach. The word in the Greek for stomach can used for the entire abdomen, the womb, the intestinal tract, or metaphorically, the innermost part of man where the will, emotion, the seat of thought or the heart of man are. This is a metaphoric expression of the intensity and burden that John was given by God in terms of his prophetic mission in writing the Revelation. As we observe the vision John wrote called the Book of Revelation, we find it is very intense in terms of visions of God and Jesus, the judgments of God, the spiritual warfare, the descriptions of the angelic order, and many other spiritual experiences that would wear out the human intellect. John could only bear this as a grace from God.

c) This scroll empowers John with the Word of God to complete his prophetic declaration as he prophesies about the glories of the Kingdom of God and the destiny of peoples and nations.

d) The Word of God is sweet. Psalm 119 reminds us of the goodness of God's Word, and the pleasure it brings to us.

CHAPTER ELEVEN

Revelation Chapter Eleven is divided into two sections. The first section prophesies the Two Witnesses and the second section prophesies the blowing of the Seventh Trumpet, which reveals to us a wide panoramic view of the end of Salvation History.

The Two Witnesses are the most difficult section of Revelation to interpret for any eschatological system, from the futurist premillennial view to the partial preterist post-millennial view because of the identity of the two witnesses, and the complications of either trying to find their identity in history or their identity as literal persons in the futurist view. In all schools of eschatological thought, there is wide diversity of the identity of the two witnesses and almost no two commentaries from respected theologians agree.

We will approach the interpretation of this section of Scripture within the confines of the symbolism they represent, refraining from an attempt to identify them as individuals in the past or in the future. What we do know is that the Scriptural symbolism is reliable because it is rooted in previous mentions in the Old Testament, and the symbols themselves communicate deep theological truths which we can apply today. As we have learned in earlier chapters, the Book of Revelation is clearly a book of Old Testament symbols that communicated spiritual truths which would have been easily understood by the First Century Christians it was written to.

We will complete the brief interlude of the Mighty Angel with the Little Scroll, the Two Witnesses, and the rest of Chapter Eleven with the finality of the Seventh Trumpet in verses 15-19.

As we mentioned in previous chapters, the Book of Revelation is one narrative, told in three sections of sevens with interludes in between. It is written in a cyclical manner, communicating the same narrative from different perspectives and degrees of intensity in explanation. As we complete Chapter Eleven, we complete the second section of sevens with the blowing of the Seventh Trumpet, which reveals the glory of God at the End of the Ages.

It is important to note a cultural truth that First Century Christians who were Jewish would find significant: The blowing of the Seventh Trumpet describes the End of the Ages and the consummation of the Kingdom of God and is a direct reference to Rosh Hashanah (Feast of Trumpets). Rosh Hashanah is not only the celebration of a New Year, but the memorial of God creating mankind, as well as the hope of God being crowned King of the Universe at the Last Day with the blowing of the Shofar. With these thoughts in mind, the content of the blowing of the Seventh Trumpet would confirm the truth, mission and success of the Gospel of the Kingdom as preached by the Church would be fulfilled. This would be a tremendous encouragement to a Church who was in its infancy and struggling under the Roman and Jewish persecutions of the First Century.

Revelation 11:1-2

a) In verse 1, we have some internal evidence of an early date for the writing of Revelation. It is assumed in verses 1 & 2 that the Temple is still standing and is in use. The use of the phrase "the holy city" identifies the place as Jerusalem, also found in Revelation 11:8.

b) John's reed/measuring rod is a symbol for testing or summing up the value of something. The measure of something establishes its dimensions and value.

c) We see a distinction between the outer and inner courts of the Temple. The outer court was destined to be destroyed, but the inner court was protected from destruction. The outer court represents the Temple in Jerusalem, and the inner court the Church in dwelt by the Holy Spirit. The Book of Hebrews deals with this in detail.

d) 42 months – This time frame corresponds directly with the time frame the Romans sieged Jerusalem.

Revelation 11:3

a) These two witnesses have been given the ability to prophesy. The words authority and power are not in the Greek but have been added by our translators. The word in the Greek is DIDMI – to give, to bestow a gift. The Greek word for witness is – MARTYS – a legal witness

b) Sackcloth – This is the clothing of prophets who were calling Israel to repentance. Sackcloth was black wool cloth and very uncomfortable. It was a used to identify the prophet and his mission. Both Elijah and John the Baptist wore this type of covering. Sackcloth was also worn when fasting and mourning as well. The reference to this prophetic garment gives us a clue that the mission of the two witnesses is to prophesy against the disobedient and those who reject the message of the Lord.

c) Again, we see the 42 month, or the 3.5 year, reference which corresponds to the time frame of the siege of Jerusalem.

Revelation 11:4-6

a) In verses 4-6, we see direct references to Zechariah 4:14, references to the ministry of Elijah and references to the ministry of Moses.

b) Zechariah 4 – the two lampstands and olive trees in Zech. 4 are Zerubbabel, the governor and Joshua, the High Priest. Zerubbabel laid the foundation of the Second Temple; Joshua re-established and presided over the altar of the Second Temple. They are symbols of authority and government.

c) Verse 5 uses the symbolism of fire from their mouths. This speaks of the symbolism of the power of the Word of God. *(See Isaiah 30:27, Jeremiah 5:14 and Jeremiah 23:29)* To disobey the Word of the Lord in terms of rejecting God's grace, all will die by that fire.

d) The reference to Elijah in being able to shut up the sky speaks of the witness of powerful prophetic words that confirm God's message. We can also see John the Baptist's ministry in view here. Jesus said John was the Elijah to come.

e) The reference to Moses speaks again of powerful prophetic ministry and judgment of God on Egypt who was rebelling against the will of God by not setting the Israelites free.

f) From simply interpreting the symbolism found in verses 4-6, we would say the Two Witnesses represent the whole sum of the Old Testament prophets until John the Baptist and their ministries to Israel. These Two Witnesses form a panoramic view of the Law and the Prophets.

Revelation 11:7-10

a) The Beast from the Abyss – This is the first mention in Revelation of the beast. This is none other than Satan and his hateful persecution of the prophets of God. Jesus said that all the blood of the prophets who were killed in Jerusalem would be on the generation that condemned Him. *(See Matthew 23:34-35)*

b) Beasts also speak of the pagan nations who attacked Israel. *(See Isaiah 1:9 & Daniel 7:3-8)*

c) Jerusalem is now called Sodom, which symbolizes its complete slide from being the dwelling place of God to the being given over to absolute wickedness that demands judgment. The city who rejected its own Messiah now must accept the consequences of her actions. *(See Matthew 23:37-39 & Luke 13:33)*

d) Jerusalem is now being called Egypt, which symbolizes its rebellion against God. Egypt was the place of bondage for God's Covenant people. Jerusalem was now a place of bondage for rejecting the freedom from the Law that Jesus offered.

e) These Two Witnesses reflected the sacrifice of Jesus, in that they were lesser sacrificial lambs, who were sacrificed for their prophetic witness to Jerusalem just like Jesus was.

f) There is often a prideful celebratory spirit that inhabits those who throw off the Law of God. It manifests in our culture as a "party spirit" that celebrates sin and loves pleasuring the flesh (SARX).

g) There was celebration at the death of John the Baptist, and Pilate and Herod also became friends after they presided over the death of Jesus.

h) Being denied burial was a sign of disrespect for the life of someone. *(See Psalm 79)*

Revelation 11:11-12

a) Again, we see a parallel to Jesus as He was resurrected and ascended to heaven. Many commentators point to the fact that the whole of the Church will be resurrected and ascend into heaven to meet Jesus Christ.

b) The reference to the sacrificial deaths of the Two Witnesses for their testimonies and their resurrection and ascension can be symbolic of the whole sum of God's people from beginning to end.

c) David Chilton writes, "The story of the Two Witnesses is therefore the story of the witnessing Church, which has received the divine command to "Come up here!" and has ascended with Christ into the clouds of heaven, to the Throne (Eph. 1:20-22; 2:6;

Heb. 12:22-24): She now possesses an imperial grant to exercise rule over the ends of the earth, discipling the nations to the obedience of faith (Matt. 28:18-20; Rom. 1:5)."

d) We need to adopt a theology of victory when we look at disasters, persecutions and crucifixions because being in Christ demands victory. Our deaths, either in distress or in peace, still speak victory because Jesus holds the keys of death and Hades.

Revelation 11:13-14

a) The symbolism of the earthquake speaks of the power of God's authority and His ability to shake what can be shaken.

b) 7000 – Seven the number of completeness – Seven multiplied to 7000 speaks of the utter destruction of those who disobeyed the testimony of the Law, the Prophets, Jesus Christ and the Witness of the Church. We see 7000 being used as a symbolic number when Elijah questioned the Lord and complained that he was the only one left who had not gone astray.

Summary

As we can see in verses 1-14, the subject of the Two Witnesses is difficult to harmonize with the previous ten Chapters, as well as the rest of the Revelation. Considering all the Scriptural symbolism of Chapter Eleven, I would present the Two Witnesses most likely do not represent two literal people but are a composite sketch of the whole of the prophetic ministry of the Hebrew prophets declaring the soon coming judgment of God on Jerusalem. An alternative explanation is that the Two Witnesses represent the ministries of Moses and Elijah in the sense that Moses represents the Old Covenant and Elijah represents the Prophets that prophesy Jesus Christ and the Law He fulfilled.

Revelation 11:15-19

a) Seventh Trumpet corresponds not only to Rosh Hashanah, but to 1 Thessalonians 4:16-18. These verses encourage us that the Lord's Day is a day of glory for the Church in which we should look forward to, not fear. So much of our eschatological thought is negative regarding the Second Coming of Jesus Christ. From the partial preterist perspective we look back in history to see the negative prophecies of Jesus as being fulfilled, and we look forward to the End of Ages as a glorious day where all things are summed up in Jesus Christ.

b) Loud voices – MEGAS PHONE – Greek – a sound or tone of an instrument or the sound of uttered words.

c) The kingdom of the world – Interestingly enough, GE – Earth – is not used here, but the Greek word KOSMOS is used. KOSMOS refers to the whole of God's creation or the whole of the created order. We worship the transcendent Creator God Almighty!

d) We see a transfer of the kingdom of the world, becoming the Kingdom of our God. This speaks of the complete redemption of the whole of creation and Eden restored. Jesus being the Second Adam rightly has dominion over all creation.

e) Verse 15 supports Trinitarian Theology and presents Jesus Christ as the Davidic King who rules forever. Jesus will reign for eternity. The Eternal Kingdom is unending bliss with no opportunity for an interruption.

Revelation 11:16

a) The 24 elders seated on their thrones around the Throne of God unseat themselves and worship God. All powers, authorities, rulers, principalities, and people fall down on their faces in the very presence of God. *(See Philippians 2:10-11)*

b) Greek – PROSKYNE – verb – to kiss the hand, to worship, give reverence, to kneel down, to bow down, and to pay homage and obeisance.

c) Revelation gives us a glimpse into the heavenly realms of angelic worship, and the worship of the redeemed. The revelation of Jesus Christ causes us to worship Him as He is worthy, and His revealing clearly shows us His excellences which cause us to respond with no regard for ourselves. The heavenly elders actively unseated themselves from their thrones, fell down and worshiped God with their spiritual bodies, and with their voices.

d) Unlocked hearts worship extravagantly like angels.

Revelation 11:17

a) We give thanks – Greek – verb – EUCHARISTE – to be grateful, and to give thanks. All worship has the element of thankfulness. The elders are thankful for the full manifestation of the God's power and reign.

b) From the earliest mentions in Church history, communion was called the Eucharist. We would be short-sighted not to see the connection here of how the Church celebrates the Body and Blood of Jesus with thankfulness, and we marvel at the redemption of the world through His sacrifice on the cross. We have been crucified with Christ, raised with Him, and will ascend at the time of His cosmic judgments at the End of the Age!

c) The Threefold Name of God – Lord – Greek – KYRIOS – he to whom a person or thing belongs, about which he has power of deciding; master, lord, the possessor and disposer of a thing,

d) God – Greek – THEOS – The Godhead

e) Almighty – Greek – PANTOKRATOR – He who rules over everything – Omnipotent

f) To summarize, we see the following things in the description of our God: He is the One we belong to, the Lord, He is the God-head, the One and Only, He is Ruler of all things. These names alone should impart fearlessness in our lives no matter the situation we face.

g) He has great power – MEGAS DYNAMIS – total power not only in terms of strength but in terms of the supernatural, and excellency of soul

h) He has begun to reign – BASILEU – to be king, to exercise kingly power, to reign, metaph. to exercise the highest influence, to control

Revelation 11:18

a) In the first part of verse 18, we are reminded of Psalm 2 and the foolishness of those who rage against God, choosing their own paths instead of His loving paths and eternal care.

b) Judging the dead – This occurs at the end of the age. *(See Revelation 20:11-15)*

c) The believers are not raised to a judgment, but to a reward.

d) To destroy those who destroyed the land – This not only speaks of the Land (Promised), but all land that is destroyed by the effects of unrighteousness. Sin not only causes a spiritual destruction on the land, but manifests as crime, tyranny, social injustice, and all things that do not reflect the blessings of the Kingdom of God.

Revelation 11:19

a) We see the True Temple in Heaven and the True Ark of the Covenant revealed to us. Unstoppable power and authority emanate from it. Flashes, thunder, lightning and hail all are metaphors for the power and authority of God.

b) The destruction of the temple in Jerusalem did not end the concept of the Covenants of God, but confirmed the New Covenant which more fully reflects His heart, as it is the fullness of His Covenant between man and God.

c) To quote David Chilton, "The early Christians who first read the Book of Revelation, especially those of a Jewish background, had to understand that the destruction of Jerusalem would not mean the end of covenant or Kingdom. The fall of old Israel was not "the beginning of the end." Instead, it was the sign that Christ's worldwide Kingdom had truly begun, that their Lord was ruling the nations from His heavenly throne, and that the eventual conquest of all nations by the armies of Christ was assured. For these humble, suffering believers, the promised age of the Messiah's rule had arrived. And what they were about to witness in the fall of Israel was the end of the Beginning."

CHAPTER TWELVE

Chapter Twelve begins another interlude between the Trumpet and the Bowl judgments. As John continues his vision in Chapter Twelve, we are introduced to the wide panoramic view of the whole of salvation history, the glory of the Church, the victory of Messiah, and the sure defeat of Satan and his demons by the angelic forces of heaven and the preaching of the Church.

This is an exciting section of Scripture, as the symbolism and allegory of spiritual realities and Biblical history are so rich. Although we may not unpack all of the glory in these verses due to the sheer volume of it, my intention here is to stir your hunger to seek the Lord to gain illumination and revelation for yourselves.

I want to continue to remind us that the book of Revelation is one narrative told in three sections of sevens, with interludes, that repeat the same narrative in increasing degrees and perspectives. I mention this so that we will begin to see the simplicity of understanding this prophetic vision. We should be encouraged by the sure victory of Jesus Christ and His beautiful Bride, the Church.

Revelation Chapter Twelve completes the first section of the interlude between the Trumpet Judgments and the Bowl Judgments. Revelation Twelve contains beautiful symbolic imagery and allegory describing the defeat of Satan and his demonic armies in the high realms of heaven, and his sure defeat by those who overcome by their faithfulness to Jesus.

Revelation Chapter 12 is primarily a wide panoramic view of the spiritual warfare that rages throughout the millennia, culminating in the victory of the

Messiah and His Church. We can find tremendous comfort in knowing that we are kept, covered and protected by the Lord in all the times and seasons of our life paths. It is an important realization that the Revelation is primarily a prophecy of the authority of Jesus, the coming glory of the Church at the consummation, and the angelic worship of the Godhead in the realm of God's presence.

Revelation 12:1-2

a) The great sign of the woman in heaven – This woman is the Israel of God. That is the people of faith who made up the Old Testament Covenant community and then continued as the New Testament Church.

b) We should refer to Genesis 37:9 to help us identify her. The central theme as the people of God being referred to as a woman is common in the Scriptures. The Church is called the Bride of Christ, and the OT people of faith are referred to collectively as a Woman; Daughter of Zion; Daughter of Jerusalem, etc., in Isaiah, Jeremiah 3-4, Ezekiel 16, Lamentations 1, Hosea & Micah 4.

c) To summarize the woman is the Old Testament Covenant people who were pregnant and bringing forth the Messiah, Jesus Christ, in pain. Israel waged warfare with Satan and battled his devices to abort the Seed. Consider the following brief list of battles to try to kill the Seed of the woman who would crush Satan's head (Genesis 3:15): Cain & Abel; Corruption of Seth's bloodline leading to the Flood; Sarah almost being defiled by two kings Pharaoh and Abimelech; the struggle of the twins Esau & Jacob; the Egyptian Captivity and the destruction of the Hebrew infants;: Haman & Esther; the infants in Bethlehem murdered by Herod. It has been a strategy by the enemy to kill the Seed who would defeat him.

d) The Virgin Mary is also in view here as she was the one who conceived the Messiah by the Holy Spirit. It is interesting to note the many attempts to kill the Seed by Satan involved faithful women of God.

Revelation 12:3-4

a) The red dragon is symbolic of Satan and his illegal dominion. The seven heads, ten horns and seven crowns speak of his illegal power as a leader over the rebellious angels who followed him.

b) His tail swept a third of the stars – The stars mentioned here are symbolic of the angels who rebelled against God. We see stars as a common symbol for angels in the Scriptures. *(See Job 38:7, Jude 1:13, Revelation 1:20)*

c) The interlude vision is highlighting the reality of the enmity and spiritual warfare which surrounds the people of God and their destinies as ones who brought forth the Messiah.

d) It is still a strategy of Satan to frustrate the victory of the Church. It is our charge to bring forth the Messiah in His Second Coming by living as the Bride who made herself ready for the Bridegroom.

Revelation 12:5

a) Jesus is the Male Child who was born of the Virgin Mary and He ascended into heaven after His resurrection.

b) Psalm 2 is referenced in verse 5.

c) We see a wide panoramic view of the salvation of Jesus Christ from the Virgin Birth to the Ascension. This does not take away from the cross. The cross was much more than forgiveness of sin, healing for the soul and body, and the process of sanctification. The ascension is the institution of the enforcement of the Kingdom of God by Jesus Christ through His Church.

Revelation 12:6

a) This refers to the Church of Jerusalem that fled to Pella during the 3.5-year siege of Jerusalem. It is important to be aware there is no historical account of Christians perishing in the destruction of Jerusalem. The Christian community in Jerusalem fled to Pella at that time. They believed the prophecies of Jesus concerning the destruction of Jerusalem in Matthew 24 and fled when they saw the Roman Army surrounding Jerusalem.

b) The Church was nourished. God always cares for His people in the wilderness. The Lord cared for the Israelites in the 40 year wandering, fed them and nourished them. The Lord cared for Mary, Joseph and Jesus when they fled to Egypt from Bethlehem. The Lord sustained the Church through all of her persecutions and trials, as proved by history. The Lord will always care for His Bride.

Revelation 12:7-9

a) The vision abruptly changes and gives us another facet to the spiritual warfare surrounding the reign and rule of Messiah. This is not meant to be chronological, but to *highlight* the gradual defeat of Satan and his demons by the angels of heaven throughout the ages.

b) Michael is mentioned in Daniel 10. His name means "who is like God". He is identified as the guardian angel of the people of God.

c) Satan lost his place in heaven. This is significant because the devil has no access or place in God's realm. Jesus said He saw Satan fall. *(See Luke 10:18)* Christ has defeated the dominion, power and position of the devil by His Resurrection and Ascension to heaven.

d) Satan's mission is to lead the world astray. It is most interesting that the Greek word OIKOUMENE is used here, and not GE or KOSMOS. OIKOUMENE is used to describe the whole inhabited world. At that time, it was the whole of the Roman Empire and her farthest boundaries. The mission of the Church is to rescue nations from the enemy. The gospel of Jesus Christ is not without power! We have the clear mandate from Jesus to disciple nations as we defeat the spiritual forces of darkness with the Gospel.

Revelation 12:10

a) In verses 10-12, we are presented with wide panoramic view of the final victory of the Kingdom of God over the demon armies of the devil. I want to point out that in Revelation 12:7, Michael and his angels are on the offense, not the defense in this cosmic spiritual battle between the dragon and the angel armies of heaven. The dominion of darkness is on defense against the advancement of the Gospel and the Kingdom of God.

b) Now has come the salvation, power, kingdom and authority of God and of His Christ. Verse 10 refers to the overwhelming and decisive victory of the Kingdom of God over darkness. Below we see the definition of this victory.

c) Salvation – Greek – SOTERIA – deliverance, preservation, safety, salvation, in an ethical sense, that which concludes to the soul's safety or salvation, future salvation, the sum of benefits and blessings which the Christians, redeemed from all earthly ills, will enjoy after the visible return of Christ from heaven in the consummated and eternal kingdom of God.

d) Power – Greek – DYNAMIS – strength power, ability, power for performing miracles, moral power and excellence of soul, the power and influence which belong to riches and wealth, power consisting in or resting upon armies, forces, hosts.

e) Kingdom – Greek – BASILEIA – royal power, kingship, dominion, rule, not to be confused with an actual kingdom but rather the right or authority to rule over a kingdom, of the royal power and dignity conferred onto Christians in the Messiah's Kingdom.

f) Authority – Greek – EXOUSIA – power of choice, liberty of doing as one pleases, the ability or strength with which one is endued, which he either possesses or exercises.

g) The accuser – The name correlates to the Hebrew concept for Satan as the Accuser of God's people. The accuser has no place in heaven to bring charges against the children of God. His assignment has been to accuse humanity before God in regards to the Fall of Man and Mankind's lack of allegiance to the authority of God in their lives. Now there is no accusation in heaven, only the voice of the Mediator, Jesus Christ. *(See 1 Timothy 2:5)*

h) To summarize the theological concepts of verse 10, we see the following: The complete deliverance of God's people has come, God's power is supreme, the Kingdom of God is fully established, and the authority of Messiah is enforced.

Revelation 12:11

a) In verse 11, we have the method of defeating satanic forces. Overcame – Greek – NIKA – to conquer, to carry off the victory, come off victorious, when one is arraigned or goes to law, to win the case, maintain one's cause – The weak ones and accused ones conquer the Accuser.

b) The blood of Jesus initiates the power of salvation. Colossians 1:20 – And through Him to reconcile all things to Himself, having made peace through the blood of His cross; through Him, I say, whether things on earth or things in heaven.

c) Word of their testimony – Greek – MARTYRIA – a testifying, the office committed to the prophets of testifying concerning future events – The saints overcome by confessing Jesus Christ and His blood Covenant with them. There is no force more powerful than the New Covenant we have in Jesus Christ.

d) Not shrinking from death – Many Christians in the Apostolic Age, and in all ages of history, have been martyred, not showing fear in the face of their persecutors. The confidence to face death in the Name of Christ is to live in the reality of His love for us.

Revelation 12:12

a) The ascension of Christ instituted the displacement of the devil in heavenly realms, the beginning of the dominion of the Messianic Kingdom, and the restoration of the Eden (earth) that Satan stole through the Fall of humanity.

b) Just because Satan was cast away from heaven and defeated in the high heavenly realms of God's presence, does not prevent the enemy from operating in the earthly realms.

c) Satan operates by agreement in lower spiritual realms, and wages spiritual warfare here by getting as many to agree with him as possible. The Church is waging war for the hearts and minds of people, as people fill all areas of society and determine the way of nations by their collective agreements.

d) The devil's time is short, as compared to eternal/infinite glory of the Kingdom of God.

Revelation 12:13

a) The focus now shifts from the warfare in heaven back to the warfare of the devil against the Church/Woman. Again, we mention the early history of the Church is full of examples of persecutions from the Jews and Romans who were conduits of satanic fury against God's faithful ones. We see many examples in Acts starting with Steven, Peter, John, the Church of

Jerusalem, and Paul.

b) Notice the dragon is hurled to the Land. The persecution of the Church began in Jerusalem and then extended through the Roman Empire and finally throughout the centuries.

Revelation 12:14

a) Verse 14 is symbolic imagery that speaks of two concepts related to the goodness of God:

1) The first concept in found in Deuteronomy 32. Deuteronomy 32:10-11 – He found him in a desert land, And in the howling waste of a wilderness; He encircled him, He cared for him, He guarded him as the pupil of His eye. "Like an eagle that stirs up its nest, that hovers over its young, He spread His wings and caught them, He carried them on His pinions. – What we see is direct reference to the deliverance of God and His faithfulness to rescue His people.

2) The second concept is the protection/encircling of the Holy Spirit – Moses references the "hovering of the Spirit" over the formless void in Genesis 1:2. Verse 14 directs our attention to the ministry of the Holy Spirit as our covering.

b) Verse 14 also confirms the flight of the Church in Jerusalem who fled the invading Roman Army which Jesus prophesied would come in Matthew 24. In previous chapters, we have mentioned the "time, times and half a time" are the exact time of the siege of Jerusalem. Lastly, it is important to note that what God does in the past is always a possibility for future generations of believers. The Lord is committed to delivering His people.

Revelation 12:15-16

a) There is a twofold interpretation for verse 15. The first part of the interpretation follows the Exodus narrative in that the Pharaoh of Egypt sought to send Israel's seed into the flood of the Nile in order to slay the Seed of Messiah, and Pharaoh's attempt to drown Israel at the Red Sea. This prophetic imagery is an encouragement for the First Century Church in that the same God who delivered Israel will continue His deliverance in the New Covenant Age.

b) The second part of the interpretation is found in history. As the Church fled the invading Roman armies, the Land of Judea absorbed the satanic flood of warfare in the siege and destruction of Jerusalem. One only must read the account of this to see the satanic horrors that were released at that time. *(See George Peter Holford's – Destruction of Jerusalem)*

Revelation 12:17

a) The prophetic imagery of verse 17 draws our attention to the Church being the extension of Israel and the continuance of God's covenant people. Verse 17 highlights the spiritual warfare that rages between the New Covenant Church and the dragon.

b) It is important to note some truth about the authority of the Church. We wage war in the offensive posture as we conquer the dragon's dominion by the authority we have in Jesus Christ. As the centuries progress, the Church has displaced more darkness and brought increasing glory to God through the Gospel, to the benefit of the world. Though we may be attacked from time to time, we are the sure Victors and all our battles will end in our favor as we persevere in our faith.

CHAPTER THIRTEEN

We will begin our exegesis of Revelation Chapter Thirteen as we continue to travel through the interlude between the Trumpet and Bowl Judgments. Before we begin, it is important to define the Antichrist according to the Scriptures. So many in the Body of Christ relate "Antichrist" to Revelation Chapter Thirteen. It may be a shock to many of us to learn the word "antichrist" is not found in the entire Book of Revelation, nor is the concept of antichrist found in Chapter Thirteen.

"Antichrist" is found in the two apostolic letters of 1 & 2 John. To rightly define what antichrist is, we will look at the four verses that mention antichrist, and interpret the meaning of antichrist in that light:

> **1 John 2:18-22**
> Children, it is the last hour; and just as you heard that antichrist is coming, even now many antichrists have appeared; from this we know that it is the last hour. They went out from us, but they were not really of us; for if they had been of us, they would have remained with us; but they went out, so that it would be shown that they all are not of us. But you have an anointing from the Holy One, and you all know. I have not written to you because you do not know the truth, but

because you do know it, and because no lie is of the truth. Who is the liar but the one who denies that Jesus is the Christ? This is the antichrist, the one who denies the Father and the Son.

1. Antichrist was already in the world when John wrote this.

2. Antichrists came from the Church, and were heretics.

3. We have an anointing from the Spirit. By the Spirit we can discern error from truth. We can see Antichrists are easily recognizable to believers.

4. The Antichrist is a person who rejects the true identity of Jesus Christ as the Son/Messiah. By rejecting the Son, one denies the Father who sent Him.

5. To summarize, we see in these verses "antichrist" is a false teaching spirit and or people who teach according to this mindset.

1 John 4:1-3
Beloved, do not believe every spirit, but test the spirits to see whether they are from God, because many false prophets have gone out into the world. By this you know the Spirit of God: every spirit that confesses that Jesus Christ has come in the flesh is from God; and every spirit that does not confess Jesus is not from God; this is the spirit of the antichrist, of which you have heard that it is coming, and now it is already in the world.

> 1. Antichrist is a spirit of false prophecy which denies the Incarnation of Jesus Christ.
>
> 2. Antichrist was already in the world at the time John writes his letter, and more are coming.
>
> **2 John 1:7**
> For many deceivers have gone out into the world, those who do not acknowledge Jesus Christ as coming in the flesh. This is the deceiver and the antichrist.
>
> 1. Antichrists are false teachers and deceivers who deny the Incarnation of Jesus Christ as God in the flesh.

There are only four verses that mention antichrist and the context of these four verses teach us antichrist is a false spirit, and or a false teacher who came out of the Church, was present at that time, and denies the truth of Jesus Christ as God the Son who came in the flesh.

Early Church Father Irenaeus gives the following account: "On meeting in the public bath at Ephesus, the Gnostic heretic Cerinthus, who denied the incarnation of our Lord, John refused to remain under the same roof, lest it might fall."

John may have had this man in mind when he wrote 1 & 2 John, as John ministered in Ephesus for many years.

We do not see a futuristic person who would be possessed of the devil and rule the world at the end of the New Covenant dispensation. We can rest assured that "Antichrist," according to the Scriptures, is not characterized in Revelation 13 as the Beast.

Now that we have rightly defined the Antichrist, we are prepared to look at Revelation 13 to interpret this chapter considering Biblical symbolism, allegory and cultural context. Chapter Thirteen is divided into two sections. Verses 1-10 define the "generic" Beast, and verses 11-18 define the "specific" Beast. We will unpack this in great detail as we interpret this chapter verse by verse.

The identity of the beast is probably the most widely discussed and hypothesized figure in modern Christianity. Every person in the Body of Christ for the last two centuries who proposed someone as the Beast of Revelation 13 has been wrong. This type of conjecture and accusation has robbed the Church of our voice to influence culture and has robbed us of the opportunity to have reasonable conversations with intelligent unbelievers looking for spiritual answers about God.

The type of sensational theories Futurist teachers of eschatology propose regarding the identity of the Beast make for good fictional stories and movies to excite the Body of Christ by focusing our attention on thoughts that the Beast is right around the corner.

However, a good look at Church History and the writings of the Early Church fathers teach us the identity of the Beast was widely known. Commentary after commentary regarding Revelation 13 are all in agreement on the identity of the Beast. In fact, Revelation 13:18 identifies the Beast by name.

David Chilton documents this fact in his commentary, *Days of Vengeance*: "It is significant that 'all the earliest Christian writers on the Apocalypse, from Irenaeus down to Victorinus of Pettau and Commodian in the fourth, and Andreas in the fifth, and St. Beatus in the eighth century, connect Nero, or some Roman emperor, with the Apocalyptic Beast'. There should be no reasonable doubt about this identification. St. John was writing to first-century Christians, warning them of things that were "shortly" to take place. They were engaged in the most crucial battle of history, against the Dragon and the evil Empire which he possessed. The purpose of the Revelation was to comfort the Church with the assurance that God was in control, so that even the awesome might of the Dragon and the Beast would not stand before the armies of Jesus Christ."

Lastly, it is important to remember that the Revelation was written to seven real Christian communities who would have been able to read it, understand it, and be encouraged by its prophecies concerning the defeat of the devil, the Roman Empire, the destruction of the Temple, the end of the Old Covenant, and the confirmation of the New Covenant. Another historical perspective to keep in mind is that John wrote this prophecy while on Patmos and this letter would have had to been carried off the island by Roman soldiers. In light of that, the Holy Spirit would have given John the Revelation in a "code" that would have been understood by a First Century believer. *(See Revelation 1:1-9)*

In previous chapters, we have learned that the Revelation is one narrative told in three sections of sevens and is repetitive, telling the same narrative from different spiritual perspectives and intensity. Much of the Book of Revelation is understood by correctly interpreting the spiritual symbols and themes through the lens of the Old Testament.

Revelation 13:1

a) The dragon standing on the shore of the sea speaks in symbolic terms of Satan having a dominion over the mass of humanity, and of him being the spirit of disobedience that inspires tyrannical and ungodly governments of nations.

b) We see the Beast mentioned again in Revelation 17, and the seven heads are descriptive language of the seven mountains of Rome. *(See Revelation 17:9)* The heads also speak of heads of government as we will see in verse 3.

c) The ten heads with blasphemous names are symbolic of the provinces of Rome spread out over the entirety of the Roman Empire. Ten is also a number of ranking, which describes the depth of rebellion against God that existed in the Roman political system.

d) These provinces were ruled by vassal kings who pledged allegiance to the Roman Emperor Herod the Tetrarch was the vassal king of Judea at the time of Jesus Christ's crucifixion.

e) Each having a blasphemous name speaks of their involvement in the false cultic religions that either worshiped the Roman Emperor, and the many cults of the Roman Empire that denied the teachings of Christianity.

Revelation 13:2

a) The Christian Community of the First Century would be

immediately reminded of Daniel 7:17. John's readers would have easily equated these symbols as empires that were symbolized by these animals. They would have easily identified the last beast as the Roman Empire. These four beasts were a continuation of Nebuchadnezzar's statue in Daniel 2. The statue represented the empires of Babylon, Medo-Persia, Greece, and Rome.

b) We can see the Roman Empire incorporated all the unrighteous power of these previous empires. It was empowered by the devil and was allied with his dominion of darkness.

c) History tells us that the Roman Empire was the most powerful empire which has ever existed in the history of the world in terms of its military power, economy, and the diversity of peoples it ruled over. The Roman Empire was truly a One World Government which had never been seen before or since its fall. The Roman Empire truly exercised great authority.

Revelation 13:3

a) Verse 3 speaks of the political turmoil in the Roman Empire at that time. Revelation 17:9-10 – Here is the mind which has wisdom. The seven heads are seven mountains on which the woman sits, and they are seven kings; five have fallen, one is, the other has not yet come; and when he comes, he must remain a little while.

b) John is speaking to First Century believers who would have easily identified these kings with the Julian-Claudian dynasty of Roman Emperors. Here is the list: Julius Caesar, Augustus, Tiberius, Caligula, Claudius, and Nero.

c) Nero is the head with the fatal wound. When Nero committed suicide, the line of the Julian-Claudian Dynasty died. Immortal Rome descended into a season of terrible civil wars until

Vespasian assumed the Throne and healed the Roman Empire that seemed to have suffered a mortal wound. We will look at Nero in much more detail as we begin to deal with the identity of the "specific" Beast in verses 11-18.

d) It is important to note that Nero's persecution of Christians lasted 42 months. November 64 AD – June 8, 68 AD

Revelation 13:4

a) From the time of Julius Caesar until the time of Nero, Roman Emperors were worshiped as gods, and were considered to be of a divine nature. Worshiping a Roman Emperor is the same as worshiping the source of their power - who is the dragon.

b) Rome was considered an immortal kingdom, as it was feared by all nations. Rome was revered as a marvel. No nation made war with Rome, as Rome was the conqueror, not the conquered.

Revelation 13:5-7

a) As we mentioned before, Nero ruled for 42 months and was the first Roman Emperor to make war against the Christians through persecution. Nero beheaded Paul, crucified Peter, and burned a large portion of Rome to the ground while blaming the Christian Community for the fire. He also did other horrible things to believers which we will detail shortly.

b) Nero was commonly called "The Beast" by the Roman Senate, as he ruled with a cruel sword, and was known for his tyranny.

Revelation 13:8

a) The religion of the Roman Empire revolved around a pantheon of gods, including the Roman Emperor. All Roman citizens were cultured into Roman customs and religion as they conquered territories and people groups.

b) Only true salvation and worship belong to the Lord.

Revelation 13:9-10

a) John is not prophesying doom to the church, but rather he is communicating that some were going to endure the hardest of persecutions, and some would even die for their Lord Jesus Christ.

b) Supernatural perseverance and faithfulness is required for such times when evil men attack God's Bride.

Revelation 13:11

a) In Verse 11, we see one who is described as a false Christ–Shepherd. It was common knowledge at that time for the Caesars of Rome to be called "King of Kings and Lord of Lords." The Roman Caesar was worshiped as being of a divine nature throughout the Roman Empire.

b) Christians believe Jesus Christ is King of Kings and Lord of Lords. These titles can only be reserved for our true King, Jesus Christ.

c) The interpretation of Verse 11 teaches us that a false Christ–Shepherd has come forth, who assumes the identity of a savior, but whose words reveal his true nature.

Revelation 13:12

a) Verse 12 continues to highlight Emperor worship which was imposed throughout the entire Roman Empire, and even into Judea.

b) In previous verses, we learned the fatal wound was the short period of time during the Roman civil wars after the death of Nero to the time when Vespasian, being of different dynasty than Nero, revived the Roman Empire by becoming Emperor, thus exerting and re-establishing Roman rule.

c) The Roman historian Tacitus writes concerning that period: "The history on which I am entering is that of a period rich in disasters, terrible with battles, torn by civil struggles, horrible even in peace. Four emperors failed by the sword; there were three civil wars, more foreign wars and often both at the same time.... In Rome there was more awful cruelty.... Besides the manifold misfortunes that befell mankind, there were prodigies in the sky and on the earth, warnings given by thunderbolts, and prophecies of the future, both joyful and gloomy, uncertain and clear. For never was it more fully proved by awful disasters of the Roman people or by indubitable signs that gods care not for our safety, but for our punishment."

Revelation 13:13

a) In verse 13, to be intellectually honest, we must admit that "great and miraculous signs" is not in the Greek text as some of our modern translations read. The Greek reads MEGAS SEMEION, which means a "great sign, mark, token or that by which a person or a thing is distinguished from others and is known." I mention this so that, being intellectually honest, we can see the Greek word SEMEION does not necessarily imply a supernatural sign.

b) It is historically important to note that Nero commanded the 12th Roman Legion to participate in the siege of Jerusalem. The word for earth in the Greek is GE and generally is used to describe a localized area, not the globe. The 12th Roman Legion was named FULMINATA which means "Armed with Lightning-Fire" and their ensign is a lightning bolt with an arrow tip at the end. Titus, who sieged Jerusalem, was one of the first Generals in military history to rain fire from the sky using war machines. The 12th Legion was famous for sending fire from the sky on their enemies as part of their battle array. This would have been the first time in history fire was used on a mass scale to siege a city.

Revelation 13:14-15

a) After Titus had captured the Temple Mount, he presided over the worship of the Image of Vespasian, defiling the Temple and then proceeded to kill all the remaining Jews by the sword.

b) The inhabitants of the land were deceived by Rome as they offered their allegiance to Rome and not to God. In John 19:15, the whole Jewish leadership and all those present at Jesus Christ's sentencing by Pilate proclaim their allegiance to the Beast (Rome).

Revelation 13:16-17

a) In the First Century, the marketplace was called the Agora. This was a place where all the services, shopping, banking, legal matters, buying and selling was conducted. At the entrance of the Agora was a statue image of the Roman Emperor, who currently was Nero. The only way to enter the Agora, was to offer a sacrifice to the Roman Emperor in order to enter (similar to paying an entrance fee). To distinguish one had offered his worship (paid to get in), he received a mark of ashes on the right hand or on the forehead. This act of worshiping Nero allowed him to enter the Agora so he could buy or sell.

b) It is important to note that John was writing to First Century Christians who would be tempted to compromise their faith by "cheating" Christ the worship He deserved in order to buy or sell.

c) The Christian community really struggled with this matter. Paul touched on this very subject in 1 Corinthians 8.

d) John was giving the Church a clear warning to not compromise in their devotion to Jesus Christ.

Revelation 13:18

a) John clearly gives the reader of Revelation the specific identity of who the Beast is by naming him in code: 666. The Greek text clearly says the name is a number "of a man," not the number "of man."

b) Caesar Nero in Hebrew adds up to 666. The Hebrew spelling of the name Nero Caesar was NRWN QSR (English Transliteration).
N = 50 + R = 200 + W = 6 + N = 50 + Q = 100 + S = 60 + R = 200 = 666

c) In many manuscripts of the Book of Revelation, the number 616 is either in the margin, or in the body of the text. If one transliterates Caesar Nero in Latin, the name adds up to 616. This was done so that a believer who is not familiar with the Hebrew language could still discern the number of the Beast - which is 666 - and is identified with Nero.

d) It was common knowledge Nero was nicknamed "The Beast" by the Romans. Here are some very disgusting facts about Nero, the Beast: Nero dressed up like an animal/beast and tortured naked Christians, even mauling their private parts with his teeth. Nero kicked his pregnant wife to death, and murdered his mother. Nero then castrated a 10-year-old boy named Sporus and married him. Nero raped Christian men and women. He burned Rome to the ground and blamed the fire on the Christians to begin his bloody persecutions. Nero covered Christians in pitch/tar and set them on fire in order to light his palace gardens at night. There are many more crimes against humanity Nero perpetrated, but this short list is enough to see his base character, therefore, we will move on.

e) It is easy to see the number 666 is Nero, and he exemplified the true nature of his father, the Dragon.

Summary

Considering real history in the context of the times during the First Century, we can rest assured knowing "The Beast" and "The Mark of the Beast" are in the past; they are defeated. We need not fear a future of facing a satanic inspired Beast with his persecutions.

It is time for the Church to transcend eschatologies that give no hope for the future. It takes away our true mission, which is to overcome all kingdoms by the Gospel of Jesus Christ. We – the Church – are to transform society into the image of our Lord and Savior, Jesus Christ.

CHAPTER FOURTEEN

In Revelation Chapter Fourteen, we continue with the interlude between the Trumpet and the Bowl Judgments. This chapter is a mega-view of the whole of salvation history from the Apostolic Church of Jerusalem to the Judgment of Jerusalem in AD 70, and the sure demise of the Roman Empire which is symbolized as the embodiment of Babylon. We see this common theme throughout the Revelation of telling and re-telling the same narrative. Revelation can be outlined as a narrative of three sections of seven's with interludes in-between.

The outline of Revelation Chapter Fourteen is as follows:

1) The First Fruits of Gospel: The Jerusalem Church – Rev 14:1-5
2) The Proclamation of the Gospel to the Nations – Rev 14:6-7
3) The Declaration of the Fall of Babylon (Roman Empire/World Systems) – Rev 14:8
4) The Judgment of Disobedience to the Gospel – Rev 14:9-12
5) The Encouragement and Promise of Rest to the Saints – Rev 14:13
6) The Reaping of the Land for Judgment – Rev 14:14-20

Revelation 14:1

a) The 144,000 are previously mentioned in Revelation 7. The 144,000 are the faithful Jews who believed in Jesus as He ministered and demonstrated that He was Messiah, or believed in Jesus through the ministry of the Apostles in Jerusalem. *(See Acts 2, Acts 3, Acts 4, Acts 5, Acts 6, Acts 7, Acts 8, and Acts 15.)*

This is not a literal 144,000 but a symbol of the many Jews who received Jesus as Messiah.

b) Romans 10-11 describes the First Fruits Community that we see in Verses 1-5.

c) The spiritual message of the imagery can be understood in the following ways: The Lamb = Jesus Christ. Jesus Christ the slain Lamb, the fulfillment of the Passover symbols who delivers His people from death. This assembly stands before Him positioned in the place of worship and they are objects of His love. The symbol of the Lamb standing on Mount Zion is figurative language which speaks of Jesus in the Place of Victory.

d) Mount Zion – This should not be understood as the literal Mount Zion, but it is best understood as the Mountain of God; the chosen place where His presence dwells; the heavenly Zion. These First Fruits of the Remnant have a special place in heaven where they behold Jesus in glory and worship Him. Interestingly enough, Zion means a "parched place" in Hebrew. If the place where God dwells is a parched place, then that would speak to the thirst His people have for Him. A heart who seeks God, deeply longing for the eternal blessings He gives is a thirsty one. Only the thirsty and the hungry get satisfied. (See Hebrews 12)

e) Having His Name and the Name of the Father on their foreheads – This symbolizes the true mark of ownership as contrasted to the mark of Beast in Revelation 13, which leads to destruction. In fact, all believers are sealed with the Spirit and kept by the Holy Spirit. *(See Ephesians 1:13; 4:30)*

Revelation 14:2-3

a) This worship of the First Fruits Church is more than just a song; it is a sound of worship, a sacred song only the Apostolic Church in Jerusalem would know as they were the ones who stayed true in the Jewish persecution of the brothers. *(See John 15:18-25)*

b) The song is unique to them, as songs are birthed from experience and understood in the place of encounter. The First Century Judean Church experienced the ministry of Jesus Christ and the Apostles in a way that could never be repeated. They experienced as eyewitnesses the ending of the Law, the giving of the New Covenant, the Holy Spirit coming at Pentecost, the unity of love, and the brutal persecution of those who rejected Messiah and scattered them. These are the redeemed of the earth (GE), the Land of Judea, not the globe (OIKUMENE).

c) We see them in the throne room where the four living creatures and the elders worship in Revelation Chapter 4.

Revelation 14:4-5

a) These are not literal virgins who are males, as the Church is made up of male and female disciples. This is best understood as those who kept themselves in purity of faith. Greek – PARTHENOS – a man who has abstained from all uncleanness and whoredom attendant on idolatry, and so has kept his chastity.

b) They follow the Lamb – This is symbolic language which speaks of their faithful journeys as faithful followers of Jesus in every season of faith. This is beautiful poetic language that describes the perseverance of the saints.

c) These were purchased – The blood of Jesus is the AGORAZO for the redeemed. *(See 1 Peter 1:18-19)*

d) No lie in their mouths – The Gospel is truth. This first generation of the Judean Church proclaimed the gospel in fullness by signs, wonders, miracles and word. The message of Jesus Christ is the Word of Life that delivers all from the dominion of darkness unto eternal life. The blood of Jesus makes us blameless. *(See Colossians 1:13)*

Revelation 14:6-7

a) In verse 6, we see the Eternal Gospel that stands as a

proclamation which began in Judea and will continue to be proclaimed to every generation until the return of Jesus Christ.

b) The angel is flying in mid-air/mid-heaven – In some way, the angelic order has a part to play in the proclamation of the Gospel by the Church. Somehow the angelic order, the Holy Spirit, and the Church work in unity to propagate the Gospel. It is interesting to note the mid-air speaks of the expanse of the atmosphere of planet earth and not OURANOS, the highest heavens where God dwells. The Gospel redeems this realm because this realm is in need of the restoration that comes by the Gospel.

c) God desires all humankind to worship Him, as He is the Source and Sustainer of all creation. *(See Romans 1:18-25)*

d) The hour of Judgment is the destruction of Jerusalem and the coming judgment at the end of the ages when Jesus Christ returns. In the epochs of salvation history, this is the last hour as there is no other "Covenant of Work of God" that needs to be done. Jesus said, "It is finished." The finished work of Jesus on the cross inaugurated the last hour.

Revelation 14:8

a) Babylon was a metaphor for the Roman Empire in the First Century. 1 Peter 5:13 is a good reference to see this point.

b) Babylon also represents the totality of the corrupt world systems of government, economy, sciences, arts, etc., that do not regard the leadership of God or Godly principles of life.

c) The dominion of darkness is doomed to fall because it is an illegal institution which was born in the Fall of mankind.

d) The Roman Empire made all the civilized world at that time drink the wine of her adulteries including: Emperor worship, gross immorality, spiritual adultery, her luxurious economy, and her tyranny of government.

e) The wine of passion/maddening of the world systems is devoid of peace and cannot bring any healing. The word for adulteries is PORNEIA in the Greek and can be defined as all illicit sex and spiritual adultery against God. Sex and spiritual adultery are married because human sexuality is sacred and is deeply tied to the spirit and soul of people.

f) It is the mission of the Church to displace Babylon and bring the superior systems of God's Kingdom to society. Babylon is already defeated because the King is enthroned and has empowered His Church to conquer in love by the Holy Spirit. The angelic order has made God's decision for the Fall of Babylon to be decreed.

Revelation 14:9-11

a) In verse 9, we continue in the progressive angelic announcements declaring the power and might of the Gospel and the decree of the fall of Babylon. This third angel decrees the eternal punishment of those who choose to worship the beast. We will need to look back at Revelation 13 for the context of the Mark of the Beast mentioned in verse 9.

b) As previously stated from Chapter 13:16, in the First Century, the marketplace was called the Agora. This was a place where all the services, shopping, banking, legal matters, buying and selling was conducted. At the entrance of the Agora was a statue image of the Roman Emperor, who at this time was Nero. The only way to enter the Agora, was to offer a sacrifice to the Roman Emperor in order to enter (similar to paying an entrance fee). To distinguish one had offered his worship (paid to get in), he received a mark of ashes on the right hand or on the forehead. This act of worshiping Nero allowed him to enter the Agora so he could buy or sell.

c) We have a "generic" beast and a "specific" beast. The generic beast is the Roman Empire and the specific beast is Nero, who is the number of a man - - 666.

d) Drinking the wine of the wrath of God is poetic language describing the effects of being drunk with deception, rebellion and spiritual blindness which is present in all who choose to reject grace.

e) Notice the mark of the beast is contrasted to the redeemed who have the name of the Father and the Lamb written on their foreheads. The symbolism speaks of our identities and who we belong to. *(See Romans 8:6-8)*

f) Being tormented with burning sulfur is spiritual symbolism describing the eternal judgment of the enemies of the gospel. The symbolism comes from Genesis 19 in the destruction of Sodom and Gomorrah. The Middle East has large deposits of this mineral along the shoreline of the Dead Sea that can burst into flames when gasses in the earth are released by earthquakes. This symbolism is used throughout the OT to speak of the judgment of God. *(See Isaiah 34:9-10)*

g) Being tormented in the presence of the angels and the Lamb teach us the reality of the eternal regret of those who reject Jesus Christ as Messiah. Those who are tormented are not literally present before Jesus and the angels, because the Redeemed are before the Godhead. Being tormented in the presence of the angels and the Lamb is the reality of regret always present to the one being tormented. The Greek word for torment is BASANIZO – to test metals by the touchstone, which is a black siliceous stone used to test the purity of gold or silver. The word is also used as a metaphor for being tested and found wanting, or being tormented by the knowledge of failure. Lastly, the word is used of physical torture.

h) The last contrast we see is in verse 11. The worshipers of the beast have no eternal rest, while the worshipers of the Lamb have eternal rest. The reality of hell is one of no rest, and the torment of the mind in total regret with no way to cover shame or receive forgiveness.

Revelation 14:12-13

a) John highlights the seriousness of Christian perseverance and losing faith in any season of our lives. The Early Church needed this exhortation due to the pressure of persecution with the temptation to abandon Jesus. *(See Romans 5:3-4, Hebrews 12:1, James 1:3-4)*

b) Blessed are the dead in Christ – At the resurrection of Jesus, the righteous dead were rescued from Abraham's Bosom (Luke 16:19-31) and were brought into the presence of God. Death in the NT is always described as the body being asleep, waiting for resurrection, and the soul/spirit of a person being present with God. *(See 1 Corinthians 15, 1 Thessalonians 4:13-19, Colossians 2:5, Philippians 1:20-24)*

c) We are promised rest when we depart from the body. *(See Revelation 21:3-4)*

d) St. Athanasius said: "All the Disciples of Christ despise death; they take the offensive against it and, instead of fearing it, by the sign of the cross and by faith in Christ trample on it as on something dead. Before the divine sojourn of the Savior even the holiest of men were afraid of death, and mourned the dead as those who perish. But now that the Savior has raised His body, death is no longer terrible, but all those who believe in Christ tread it under foot as nothing, and prefer to die rather than to deny their faith in Christ, knowing full well that when they die they do not perish, but live indeed, and become incorruptible through the resurrection."

e) St Ignatius, Bishop of Antioch, who was torn by wild beasts in Rome (AD 107) said: "From Syria even unto Rome, I fight with wild beasts, by land and sea, by night and day, being bound amidst ten leopards, even a company of soldiers, who only wax worse when they are kindly treated. Howbeit, through their wrongdoings, I become more completely a disciple".

f) 1 Corinthians 15:32 – Paul testifies he survived the beasts in the Coliseum of Ephesus.

Revelation 14:14-16

a) Here we see Jesus described again as "a Son of Man". The First Century reader or hearer would be drawn to thoughts of Daniel 7:13.

b) Jesus is described as having a gold crown, which speaks of His authority to rule and have dominion, His purity and His wealth as King of Kings.

c) The sharp sickle in His hand – The Greek word used here is for a tool that vinedressers, or those who prune trees, use. Jesus is being described as the One who will punish Jerusalem for rejecting Him as true Messianic King.

d) The word for earth here in this section is GE, which describes a localized area, specifically the Land of Judea.

e) This is not a harvest unto salvation, but a harvest of judgment. Jesus said in Matthew 26:64 that the Sanhedrin would see Him come on the clouds with power. Jesus used a common metaphor for the judgment of God when He said this which is why the High Priest tore his clothes and accused Jesus of blasphemy. Jesus equated Himself as being God. Later in Matthew 27:25, the non-believing Jews confirmed their rejection of Jesus by saying, "Let his blood be on us and our children!" This is a chilling declaration as the blood of Jesus holds the power to save or to condemn.

f) In AD 67-70, the Land was ripe for harvest as God used the Roman Army to destroy the Land and the Temple.

Revelation 14:17-18

a) Again, we see the angelic order having a ministry in decreeing God's decisions, aiding in ministry to the Godhead and helping the saints. In this case, we see decree and ministry to God. It is interesting to note that there is an angel assigned to keeping the fire burning on the altar before the throne.

b) In the OT, priests kept the fire burning on the altar in the Temple. Today believers have the eternal flame of the Spirit on the altars of our hearts, and in heaven the angelic realm tends the true Temple of God. Revelation is a beautiful prophetic vision that truthfully describes the unseen spiritual realms and the eternal dwelling of God in heaven (OURANOS).

Revelation 14:19-20

a) The Vineyard is a metaphor for Israel in the OT. *(See Isaiah 5:1-7)* What we are seeing in these verses is the symbolic language for the total destruction of the land who abandoned their Messiah.

b) 1600 stadia – The length of the Land of Judea. It is easy to miss this detail, as it not only describes the vast amount of bloodshed in the Land by the Roman Army, but it gives us the actual dimension of the Land from top to bottom. Vespasian and Titus shed blood from the North to the South and, in Jerusalem alone, the siege cost 1.1 million lives.

c) Outside the City – The city is Jerusalem – Hebrews 13:11-14 describes for us the spiritual symbolism of Jesus, our sacrificial Lamb, suffering outside the city in His body, and the Church of Jesus offering the sacrifice of praise "outside the city" of the Old

Covenant system of worship.

d) In AD 33, Jesus suffered outside the City. In AD 70, the Vine of Israel is cut down, trampled in the winepress of God's judgment and the Old Covenant was destroyed forever.

e) We can be sure the future does not hold mass bloodshed for the planet earth, but an ever-increasing Kingdom of God until the return of Jesus Christ.

CHAPTER FIFTEEN

The whole of Revelation Chapter Fifteen is the introduction to the Seven Bowl Judgments. This chapter is the on-ramp that invites us back into the throne room, and from that vantage point we witness the glory of God, the purity of His nature and character; and lastly, the heavenly perspective of the judgments of God. It is important to point out the judgments of God are always perfect, pure, and the very essence of them are holy. The judgments of God are never unrighteous, cruel, unjustified, or unfair.

Before we move forward, let us look at the cross to examine the judgments of God toward sin; the judgments of God in relation to the Fall; and the judgments of God on the rebellious, on Satan and on his demons:

> 1. The Judgments of God on sin: The Father imputed sin onto Jesus Christ in our behalf and judged sin through His Son. *(See 2 Corinthians 5:21)*
>
> 2. The Judgments of God in relation to the Fall: Because of the Fall, the whole created order was bound to decay, but through the redemption of Jesus Christ creation is being restored in a limited manner now, and at the coming of Christ, it will be

completely healed. *(See Romans 8:18-27)*

3. The Judgments of God on the rebellious, Satan and demons: God will judge rebellious people and Satan and his demons at the end when all things are summed up in Jesus Christ. *(See Colossians 2:13-15 & Romans 2:5-6)*

As we can see, two things are in view: The first is that God provided a way to escape judgment by coming to His Son who stood in our place and became judgment for us. Even the effects of the Fall are healed by the Son. Jesus is the remedy to the Fall regarding paying the price for sin, healing the effects of sin, healing the creation and destroying the works of the devil.

The second thing is that the Judgment occurs at the end of the age of grace/age of the New Covenant, showing us that God is patient and gives every opportunity for all to make a choice. I desire for us to see the kindness and goodness of God in relation to His judgments, because from this vantage point, we escape the opportunity to view God as punitive, angry, unloving, and harsh.

A brief outline of Revelation Chapter Fifteen is as follows:

1) The Second Sign in Heaven – The last judgments are announced – Rev 15:1
2) The Faithful before the Throne – Rev 15:2
3) The Song of Moses and The Lamb – The nature and character of God are extolled – Rev 15:3-4
4) Tabernacle in Heaven Opened – Rev 15:5
5) The Creature gives the Bowls to the Angels – Rev 15:7
6) The Temple in Heaven filled with Smoke from the Glory of God and His Power – Rev 15:8

Revelation 15:1

a) This is the second great sign in heaven that John had observed in his vision. The first was in Revelation 12. Each of these great signs sections highlight to us a macro view of spiritual truth concerning God's ability to deliver His people, judge His enemies, and display His glory. Therefore, when we hear the "great sign in heaven" language, we should expect to see a wide panoramic view concerning a spiritual concept. In this case, we observe a wide panoramic view of judgments of God on Jerusalem, Rome, and the eventually all of the systems of the world.

b) We see a snap shot here of the mission of the seven angels and the contents of their bowls. This last cycle of sevens is the most intense cycle of sevens as it gives us heaven's perspective in relation to the judgments of God. As mentioned in previous chapters, Revelation is a cycle of three sevens, separated by interludes, telling the same narrative in varying degrees of intensity and perspectives.

c) It is important to consider the context of the Greek words for "plagues" and "wrath" as this will help us interpret this chapter. Plagues – Greek – PLEGE – A blow, stripe or wound, a public calamity, or heavy affliction. We tend to view a plague as a disease. This is not the thought behind the Greek use of the word here. What is being highlighted in this verse is that God will demonstrate His discipline against everything that resists His love.

d) Wrath – Greek – THYMOS – Passion, angry, heat, anger forthwith boiling up and soon subsiding again. What we see is a God's anger being described as passionate, but short in duration. God is not petty and does not carry a grudge or judge with impunity.

e) God's wrath is finished/completed – This is not to be understood in the sense of finality, but in that these seven bowls complete the judgment cycle for Jerusalem and the Roman Empire. The final day of judgment is the Great White Throne Judgment in Revelation 20:11 where the entirety of humanity (individually) is called to account for its deeds. Greek – TELEO – verb – to bring to a close, to perform, execute, complete, fulfill, (so that the thing done corresponds to what has been said, the order, command, etc.)

f) Seven – Number of completion, finality and rest.

Revelation 15:2

a) The sea of glass mixed with fire – This language takes us back to the Throne Room in Revelation 4. This is the glorious place where the Godhead is revealed in glory, power and all the majestic beauty of our Bridegroom God.

b) The ones in view have been victorious over the following: The first victory is over the beast. This would be the generic beast of the corrupt Roman Empire. The second victory is over the idolatry of the image of the beast. This is victory over Emperor Worship, polytheism, spiritual adultery of every kind, and all idol worship or false representations of God. The third victory is over the number of the beast which is the specific beast, Nero. Nero was the first to persecute the Church of Jesus Christ, and this third victory was received by remaining faithful to Jesus in the midst of persecution.

c) God gave them harps – God empowers His worshipers when they breakthrough in victory over the evil one. God rewards each of us with the ability to worship. Worship is the weapon of believers and the boast of the Church over our enemies.

Revelation 15:3

a) The Song of Moses is found in Deuteronomy 31-34. This song is a sung narrative about the True God, His Nature and Character, His Rebellious People, and His Judgment against Them.

b) The Song of the Lamb – Revelation 5:9-10 – The song of the Lamb is a sung narrative about the redemption of the cross, the New Covenant people from every tribe and nation, their priesthood and their victory.

c) What we see is the whole story of fallen Israel/Old Covenant contrasted to the faithful First Century saints who overcame the pressures on the Early Church. We, too, are invited into this reality as we walk out our faith in our personal callings and destinies in Jesus Christ.

Revelation 15:3-4

a) Revelation 3 through 4 describe the glory of God, His purity, and position as being the only Potentate worthy of worship.

b) His deeds are marvelous – Your ways are true – Greek – HODOS – a way traveled.

c) Who will not recognize Your identity as being the Uncreated Omnipotent God.

d) He is holy – Totally set apart from His creation.

e) All people will worship Him – All will confess Him at salvation or confess Him at Judgment.

f) Everything God does is pure and righteous.

Revelation 15:5

a) The true tabernacle in heaven (the one Moses copied), is open. This is wonderful news because Christians have access to this intimate place of meeting with the Lord face to face like Moses did. This was confirmed when the veil of the temple in Jerusalem was torn in two. *(See Matthew 27:51)*

Revelation 15:6

a) These seven angels are on assignment to carry out the seven woundings/public calamities. These are priestly angels who serve in the heavenly temple. It is interesting we to continue to see the vast variety of angels, and their multi-faceted purposes.

b) The imagery of the angels describes their mission: Dressed in white – this speaks of their purity and holiness; Gold sashes around their chests – this speaks of their glory and their perfect fidelity to God.

Revelation 15:7

a) One of the living creatures gives the angels bowls – These would be like the earthly bowls that were used in the temple for pouring blood on the altar, etc.

b) These bowls contain the completion of God's judgment on those who clung to the Old Covenant and not to Jesus, as well as the destruction of Jerusalem and Rome.

c) God is described as eternal/self-existent. This is so important because as He is eternal, we become eternal by being in Him through Jesus Christ. The Eternal One has life in Himself. We can draw from that Life, and benefit from that Life through our knowledge of Him.

Revelation 15:8

a) We are reminded of 2 Chronicles 7 at Solomon's dedication of the Temple when the priests were unable to minister because of the overwhelming presence of God in the glory cloud and fire from heaven.

b) The smoke came from the glory – Greek – DOXA – magnificence, excellence, preeminence, dignity, grace, a most glorious condition, most exalted state, of that condition with God the Father in heaven to which Christ was raised after He had achieved His work on earth

c) The smoke came from the Power – Greek – DYNAMIS – strength power, ability, inherent power, power residing in a thing by virtue of its nature, or which a person or thing exerts and puts forth, power for performing miracles, moral power and excellence of soul, the power and influence which belong to riches and wealth, power consisting in or resting upon armies, forces, hosts.

d) What we see here is that even the judgments of God are glorious and display His goodness because they are rooted in truth. It was right for God to destroy the Old Covenant temple system of worship because it denied His Son and the New Covenant which He established by His blood. It was also right for God to judge the Roman Empire for the blood of the martyrs of the Early Church.

CHAPTER SIXTEEN

Revelation Chapter Sixteen begins to provide us with details of each of the Bowl Judgments in sharp, detailed figurative language which causes us to recognize the seriousness of the rejection of Messiah by the unbelieving Jews and the persecutors of the Roman Empire.

It is interesting to contrast the Bowl Judgments to the Trumpet Judgments, as the Trumpet Judgments were signified by thirds and the Bowl Judgments are described in terms of finality. This points us to the truth that the Lord God is patient and gives all people significant time to repent/change their minds about Him. 2 Peter 3:9 – The Lord is not slow about His promise, as some count slowness, but is patient toward you, not wishing for any to perish but for all to come to repentance.

It is also important for us to see the parallelism between the Lord's judgments of Egypt when He delivered the Israelites from oppression, and the Bowl Judgments in Revelation 16. This parallelism points to two truths concerning the Seven Bowl Judgment Cycle:

1. The Bowl Judgments will bring freedom for the ones being oppressed.

2. The commands/decrees of God have the power to accomplish what has been decreed or commanded. There is power and finality in His word.

The Seven Bowl Judgment Cycle of Revelation 16 is a narrative that is a wide panoramic view of the judgment of Jerusalem, and the Roman Empire. As we complete the Seven Bowl Judgment Cycle, we begin some of the most exciting prophetic spiritual imagery found in the Revelation. We will also see the end of Revelation 16 is the perfect on-ramp into Revelation 17 through Revelation 18 which details the fall of the Roman Empire and the future Babylons of the world that stand against the Kingdom and people of God in all ages.

Revelation 16:1

a) The voice from the temple in heaven is God's voice. In Revelation 15:8 we are told that the temple in heaven was filled with smoke from God's power and His glory.

b) The angels hear the command and begin to move in their ministries as deliverers of God's wrath. Greek – Wrath – THYMOS – passion, angry, heat, anger forthwith boiling up and soon subsiding again. It is important to recognize the brevity of God's anger regarding judgment. The Lord does not hold grudges, act torturously or unmercifully. The Scriptures tell us that God's anger is for a moment. Psalm 30:5 – For His anger is but for a moment, His favor is for a lifetime; Weeping may last for the night, But a shout of joy comes in the morning.

Revelation 16:2

a) The bowl judgment of the sores parallels Exodus 9:8-12. This points us to the revelation of God acting on behalf of His people as Deliverer, Avenger, and a Sovereign.

b) It is important to point out that we are interpreting spiritual symbols which are meant to point the hearer/reader to spiritual concepts and truth. It is a mistake to interpret these verses in a literal interpretation because we would completely miss the truth that is being communicated to us by the symbol.

c) I want to point our attention to the word-for-word translation of the Greek: "So the first poured out his bowl on the land and it became a loathsome and malignant sore on the people who had the mark of the beast and who worshiped his image." This is an entirely different meaning than many of our translations translate this verse. The best translation is the NASB version.

d) Land – Greek – GE – a regional, local area, arable land, etc. The land in view here is not the entirety of the planet, but the land of Judea which is being judged for its rejection of Messiah. The land became loathsome because it had become corrupt by shedding the blood of the martyrs of the Church and its Savior, Jesus Christ. Loathsome in Greek – KAKOS – of a bad nature, not such as it ought to be, of a mode of thinking, feeling, acting, base, wrong, wicked. It is irony that the land which was intended to glorify God became like Sodom. *(See Revelation 11:8)*

e) Malignant – Greek – PONEROS – Full of labors, annoyances, hardships, pressed and harassed by labors; in a physical sense: diseased or blind; in an ethical sense: evil, wicked or bad.

f) Sore – Greek – HELKOS – A wound producing puss, an ulcer.

g) The people who had the mark of the beast and his name – The Chief Priest at Jesus' trial declared he had no other king than Caesar, and the people of the land declared Jesus' blood would be on them and on their children.

h) We have a contrast between the people who swear allegiance to the beast and those who swear allegiance to the Lamb. Those who worship the Lamb have rest, presence, and eternal life. Those who worship the beast have agony and everlasting torment in the spiritual sense.

i) We can rightly summarize this verse by saying the land of Judea had become of a bad nature, wicked and not as it ought to be by turning from God and aligning itself with the inferior kingdom of Caesar. The people would suffer an incurable wound that they could not be delivered from. Josephus gives many examples in his histories of the corruption, death, and spiritual adultery of Jerusalem.

Revelation 16:3-6

a) As the second and third angel poured out their bowls, we see a parallel between this judgment and Exodus 7:17-21 when the water of the Nile turned to blood and brought death to the river. The Nile was a conduit of commerce, health and provision for Egypt. The Nile also was represented by the false God, Hapi, which was represented as an intersex being who was depicted by male and female traits.

b) Sea is a metaphor for masses of people in Scripture. *(See Genesis 32:12, Isaiah 11:9, Isaiah 57:20 & Jeremiah 6:23)* There are many other Scripture references that use the sea as a metaphor for masses of people.

c) We could interpret the symbolism of this verse by saying that this angel poured out a judgment on the mass of people who rejected Jesus Christ as Messiah, and were judged by having to give account for the blood of the righteous being shed. Matthew 23:34-36 – Therefore, behold, I am sending you prophets and wise men and scribes; some of them you will kill and crucify, and some of them you will scourge in your synagogues, and persecute from city to city, so that upon you may fall the guilt of all the righteous blood shed on earth, from the blood of righteous Abel to the blood of Zechariah, the son of Berechiah, whom you murdered between the temple and the altar. Truly, I say to you, all these things will come upon this generation.

d) It is important to note historically that during the siege of Jerusalem, the water of the city became undrinkable by the filth, dead bodies and stoppage by the Roman Army sieging it.

History gives us the account of Titus putting pressure on the water supplies going into the city and stopping the flow of fresh water.

e) Just as the blood of the oppressed Israelites in Egypt was avenged by God, so the blood of Jesus, the prophets and the faithful was avenged in the destruction of Jerusalem. The Scriptures teach us that all innocent blood will be accounted for. Psalm 72:14 – He will rescue their life from oppression and violence, And their blood will be precious in his sight; Genesis 4:10 – He said, "What have you done? The voice of your brother's blood is crying out to Me from the ground."

Revelation 16:7

a) Interestingly, the altar responds to the declaration of the angel who has charge over the waters.

b) An altar is the place where sacrifice is offered. It is a sacred place, holy and set apart for the worship of God.

c) The Old Covenant altar is devoid of life because it has been replaced by the true altar of the cross of Jesus Christ, who is the fulfillment of all Old Covenant offerings. The altar of the cross has life, therefore it speaks a better blood than any sacrifice. *(See Hebrews 12:24)*

d) The judgments of God are true – Greek – ALETHINOS – That which has not only the name and resemblance, but the real nature corresponding to the name, in every respect corresponding to the idea signified by the name, real, true genuine; opposite to what is fictitious, counterfeit, imaginary, simulated or pretended.

e) Just/Righteous – Greek – DIKAIOS – Innocent, perfect, and completely pure regarding the nature of divine law.

f) 1 John 1:5 – God is light and there is no darkness in Him.

Revelation 16:8-9

a) The fourth angel poured out his bowl on the sun. The word in the Greek – HELIOS – The sun, rays of the sun, or the light of day.

b) The Greek text does not use the phrase "power to scorch people". The text says, "and it was given it to scorch people with fire."

c) This exposure of the sun references the Exodus 13:21-22 when the Israelites were shielded from the heat of the day on their 40 year desert wanderings. Later in Scripture, the metaphor of not being harmed by the sun, or "to be shielded from the sun" is symbolism that references the blessing of being covered by the Lord under the protection of His glory cloud or the shadow of His presence. *(See Psalm 121:5-7, Isaiah 49:10, Jeremiah 17:7-8)* We can see from these verses that the clear understanding to be shielded from the sun is to be understood as metaphor.

d) In Revelation 15, we learned the Greek word for Plague – PLEGE – meant "blow, stripe, wound or public calamity," not a disease or outbreak of disease. The context of this plague is to be viewed as a punishment, per the Covenant blessings and curses in Deuteronomy 28.

e) The proper interpretation of verses 8-9 is that God's blessing and covering has been removed. The people who have rejected Messiah are openly exposed to the consequences of being outside the blessing and covering of God. Just as HELIOS references the light of day, the light of God's word can either be a blessed revelation/illumination, or it can be a light that convicts and pressures the soul with the heat of its power. Verse 9 makes it clear that as Jerusalem suffered during its destruction, the religious leadership did not repent for their crucifixion of God's Son, Jesus Christ. The Greek word for repent is METANOEO – to change one's mind, to repent, to change one's mind for better, heartily to amend with abhorrence of one's past sins. As covered in previous chapters, Josephus documented supernatural signs that took place at the Temple in Jerusalem from the resurrection of Jesus to its destruction by Titus in AD 70. These were warning signs for the Priesthood and religious leadership of Jerusalem to amend their ways before God. Even during the pressure of the siege and the pending destruction of the Temple, the Priesthood still did not consider the message the Church was preaching in Jerusalem was true.

f) At the end of the siege of Jerusalem, much of the city was consumed by fire and, specifically the Temple Mount, was burned to the ground. What was left of the Temple was broken down and plowed under just as Jesus had prophesied. *(See Matthew 24:2)*

Revelation 16:10-11

a) The next three bowl judgments are directed towards the political entities that were enemies to the Lord and His Church. The fifth bowl is directed at the throne of the beast. This is speaking of the generic beast, the Roman Empire, as well as the specific beast, Nero, who was the Roman Emperor at that time.

b) The metaphor for being darkened refers to the fall of kingdoms that are under God's judgment. We can reference Isaiah 13:9-10 (against Babylon) and Ezekiel 32:7-8 (against Egypt) as examples.

c) After the suicide of Nero in June of AD 68, the Roman Empire was leaderless and was plunged into revolution. Below are some quotes from historians concerning those darkened days. FW Farrar writes, "The horrors inflicted upon Rome and Romans in the civil wars by provincial governors – already symbolized as the horns of the Wild Beast, and here characterized as kings yet kingdomless. Such were Galba, Otho, Vitellius, and Vespasian. Vespasian and Mucianus deliberately planned to starve the Roman populace; and in the fierce struggle of the Vitellians against Sabinus and Domitian, and the massacre which followed, there occurred the event which sounded so portentously in the ears of every Roman – the burning to the ground of the Temple of the Capitoline Jupiter, on December 19th, A.D. 69. It was not the least of the signs of the times that the space of one year saw wrapped in flames the two most hallowed shrines of the ancient world – the Temple of Jerusalem and the Temple of the great Latin god." The Roman historian Tacitus who was alive during this time writes, "The whole city presented a frightful caricature of its normal self: fighting and casualties at one point, baths and restaurants at another, here the spilling of blood and the litter of dead bodies, close by prostitutes and their like – all the vice associated with a life of idleness and pleasure, all the dreadful deeds typical of a pitiless sack. These were so intimately linked that an observer would have thought Rome in the grip of a simultaneous orgy of violence and dissipation. There had indeed been times in the past when armies had fought inside the city, twice when Lucius Sulla gained control, and once under Cinna. No less cruelty had been displayed then, but now there was a brutish indifference, and not even a momentary interruption in the pursuit of pleasure."

d) The reference to men gnawing their tongues is a reference to be choking for air.

e) The interpretation of verses 8-9 is the throne of the beast, the Roman Empire at that time, was plunged into darkness, and the corrupted/ulcerous Roman society suffered for its persecution of the Church. It did not consider responding to the grace of the God in the message of the Church, but pursued its paganism.

Revelation 16:12

a) This is a wonderfully fun verse to exegete. Previously in Revelation 9:4, we learned the Northern border of Israel - the Euphrates - was always the place where the enemies of God's people would invade the land. We have examples in Scripture of the Babylonians being the enemies from the North that the Lord used to punish the land of Judea for its spiritual adultery. The prophetic books of Isaiah and Jeremiah outline these thoughts in detail.

b) In history, Cyrus and his army diverted the flow of the Euphrates and took Babylon by traveling up the riverbed on "dry ground." Other ancient armies used the same tactic to cross their massive armies over the River Euphrates.

c) It is not a coincidence that thousands of men from Titus' army came from the Euphrates to invade Judea and siege Jerusalem.

Revelation 16:13-14

a) In verse 13, we see a parallel to the plague of frogs in Exodus 8:1-7. Frogs are unclean animals to eat according to the Law, so these deceiving spirits are rightly described as unclean by the metaphor of a frog.

b) These demon frogs come from the mouth of the dragon/Satan, the mouth of the beast who is empowered by Satan (Rome and its Emperors) and the mouth of the false prophet (The High Priest and the Elders of Jerusalem) who swore allegiance to the beast in John 19:15 and declared the blood of Jesus would be on them and their children *(See Matthew 27:25)*. In this, we see Satan as a grand manipulator of the ungodly world systems. It is the mission of the Church to exert influence on these systems and bring a redemption as the salt and light of the world.

c) It is also important to note that "miraculous signs" as found in the NIV and other translations is wanting. The Greek word for signs is SEMEION – which means "a sign, mark token, or that by which a person or thing is distinguished from other and is known". What is being said here is that the message of these demons is easily seen, and their counsel unifies the wicked rulers of the age.

d) The Greek word for the "whole world" is OIKOUMENE – which means the civilized world controlled by the Roman Empire at that time, not the entire globe. At that time, the Roman Empire was ruled by the Caesar and the provinces of the Roman Empire were ruled by lesser kings. King Herod was one of them. The provinces ruled by these kings dedicated troops and resources to the conquest of Judea and Jerusalem. Josephus, in his Antiquities, documents this.

e) The day of the Lord is twofold: In Joel chapters 1 & 2, we see the Day of Lord as a reference to the invading Babylonian Army, as well as a future eschatological event. The day of the Lord is always a day of darkness, judgment and destruction. Jerusalem suffered a "day of the Lord" when it was conquered by Babylon, and suffered another one at the destruction on AD 70. The title "God Almighty" is used in Joel as well. This brings our focus to the truth that God is the only true God and Sovereign in the universe He created. We also see the Day of the Lord refers to the end of the age when Jesus returns and overthrows all un-godliness, establishing His unhindered reign on the earth. We can see this in Revelation 19.

f) What we see in verses 13-14 is a historical fulfillment and a future promise of fulfillment at the return of Jesus Christ. Paul writes about this in detail in 2 Thessalonians 2:7-12, as he describes the deception of those who reject Jesus in all ages as well as at the end of the age when He returns.

Revelation 16:15

a) Verse 15 is an interjection of the voice of Jesus to the Church to stay vigilantly awake in the place of prayer and remain aware of His presence in their lives. Jesus also makes an emphasis on the nature of His coming: suddenly and surprising. Surprising in a positive sense to those who are awake; surprising in a negative sense for those who do not consider Him.

b) Keeping clothed speaks of staying under the protective covering of Jesus Christ so that we are not exposed to the shame of unfaithfulness. Jesus used similar language when He addressed the Laodicean Church in Revelation 3:18, when He used a play on words to describe the state of spiritual unfaithfulness in the Laodicean Church. Laodicea was famous for its fine clothing.

c) It is interesting to note, those Levites who were in charge of watching over the Temple at night had their linen garments set on fire by the High Priest if they were caught sleeping twice. The metaphor for this was that one was caught unaware like being robbed by a thief in the night, and as their clothing burned they had to shed it in order to not get injured, and thus were found naked. This is a well-documented practice in the time of Jesus.

d) The thought here is that we should not be caught in a temporary state of unfaithfulness when Jesus is revealed. The verse here is not teaching an eternal condemnation for those who lapse, but a very embarrassing exposure of the shame of not being in devotion to Jesus when He returns for His Bride who should be white, clean and mature.

e) Being awake, clothed and covered with Jesus is always the place of blessing, grace and favor in our lives.

Revelation 16:16

a) When we consider the battle of Armageddon (HAR-MEGIDDO in Hebrew), we need to note that this place does not literally exist. HAR, in Hebrew, means Mountain and MEGIDDO refers to the Plain of Megiddo. There is literally no MOUNT MEGIDDO in Judea. The closest mountain adjacent to Megiddo is Mount Carmel.

b) What we have here is a play on words which the Hebrew mind would have connected to Mt. Carmel and the Plain of Megiddo.

c) Mt. Carmel is symbolic of the revelation of God to His people and the defeat of Jezebel's false prophets of Baal. *(See 2 Kings 18 for details)*

d) Megiddo is the place in the history of Israel where wars were fought, kings were judged and kingdoms either rose or fell. Here are some examples in Scripture of these concepts: Joshua 12:21 – Joshua defeated Tanaach the king of Megiddo when he lead the conquest of Canaan; Judges 5:19-20 – Deborah defeated the kings of Canaan at Megiddo; 2 Kings 9:27 – Ahaziah, the King of Judah (Ahab's disobedient grandson), was killed at Megiddo by Jehu's army. This is an example showing alliance with evil always leads to death and defeat. The last to mention is the death of Josiah in 2 Chronicles 35:20-25. Josiah had deliberately disobeyed God's command not to fight Pharaoh Neco, King of Egypt at Megiddo. Josiah was shot by an arrow in Megiddo and died from his battle wound. After his death, Judah began their decent into idolatry and the spiritual adultery that lead to their exile from the land.

e) Another notable Scripture mention is Zechariah 12:9-11 – And in that day I will set about to destroy all the nations that come against Jerusalem. I will pour out on the house of David and on the inhabitants of Jerusalem, the Spirit of grace and of supplication, so that they will look on Me whom they have pierced; and they will mourn for Him, as one mourns for an only son, and they will weep bitterly over Him like the bitter weeping over a firstborn. In that day there will be great mourning in Jerusalem, like the mourning of Hadadrimmon in the plain of Megiddo.

In these verses, we are encouraged to look forward to a future eschatological event that gives us the imagery of the mourning of Israel for rejecting Jesus as Messiah when He returns.

f) Therefore, we can see the following themes associated with Carmel and Megiddo. False prophets are defeated, evil kings are defeated, righteous prophets are promoted, righteous kings are exalted, and all the nations of earth are judged by God. Armageddon is a multi-layered symbolism for the sure defeat of the enemies of God.

Revelation 16:17

a) The Seventh Angel pours his bowl on the air. This is Divine judgment on Satan's realm of influence. Ephesians 2:2 – In which you formerly walked according to the course of this world, according to the prince of the power of the air, of the spirit that is now working in the sons of disobedience.

b) Greek – AER – the air, particularly the lower and denser air as distinguished from the higher and rarer air – The definition of this Greek word points to the reality that Satan and his demons dwell in lower heavens, not the OURANOS of God.

c) It is done! – Greek – GINOMAI – verb – to become, i.e. to come into existence, begin to be, receive being – This is the language of finality. Seven is the number of completion, rest from works, and the divine number of God. Here we see prophesied the complete destruction of the devil and his realm.

Revelation 16:18

a) Verse 18 points us the spiritual shaking of ungodly realms. Hebrews 12:25-29 – See to it that you do not refuse Him who is speaking. For if those did not escape when they refused him who warned them on earth, much less will we escape who turn away from Him who warns from heaven. And His voice shook the earth then, but now He has promised, saying, "YET ONCE MORE

I WILL SHAKE NOT ONLY THE EARTH, BUT ALSO THE HEAVEN. This expression, "Yet once more," denotes the removing of those things which can be shaken, as of created things, so that those things which cannot be shaken may remain. Therefore, since we receive a kingdom which cannot be shaken, let us show gratitude, by which we may offer to God an acceptable service with reverence and awe; for our God is a consuming fire.

b) Verse 18 details the complete shaking of everything ungodly or contrary to Him so that His kingdom may be established without hindrance. The Temple in Jerusalem was shaken in 70 AD, and at the Second Coming of Jesus, all will be shaken again as He establishes His eternal rule on earth.

Revelation 16:19

a) The Great City is a reference to Jerusalem. See Revelation 11:8 to reference the identification of the Great City.

b) The division of the Great City into three parts reminds us of the Lord's three-fold destruction of Jerusalem in Ezekiel 5:1-2 – As for you, son of man, take a sharp sword; take and use it as a barber's razor on your head and beard. Then take scales for weighing and divide the hair. One third you shall burn in the fire at the center of the city, when the days of the siege are completed. Then you shall take one third and strike it with the sword all around the city, and one third you shall scatter to the wind; and I will unsheathe a sword behind them – We see the final fulfillment of this prophecy in AD 70.

c) The cities of the Gentiles/Nations collapsed – Here is imagery which causes us to see a fulfillment in the First Century, as well as future fulfillment when all evil is defeated by God at the end of the New Covenant era.

d) God remembered Babylon the Great – This is a reference to the Roman Empire. Peter uses this idiom in 1 Peter 5:13. We know from history that the Church imputed the title of Babylon to the Roman Empire as way to connect it to the biblical historical wickedness of that city. Peter wrote the letter of 1 Peter in Rome before his crucifixion by Nero. God remembered the persecution of His people by Nero and the subsequent Roman Emperors, as well as all persecutions in every age.

e) The identity of Babylon the Great as the Roman Empire is important to us as we find the remainder of Revelation details the historical fall of Rome. Through the fall of historical Rome, we see the wider eschatological vision of the fall of the Babylon represented throughout the ages until the return of Christ.

Revelation 16:20

a) Verse 20 gives us the symbolism that nothing is ever hidden from the Lord. Just as the Roman Empire afflicted great persecutions on the Church, all acts of evil towards the people of God will be called to account by the Godhead.

b) See Revelation 6:16 – and they said to the mountains and to the rocks, "Fall on us and hide us from the presence of Him who sits on the throne, and from the wrath of the Lamb."

c) Hebrews 9:27 – And inasmuch as it is appointed for men to die once and after this comes judgment

d) We see that everything is called to account by God, which is why vengeance belongs to Him and not to us. It is important to note that all the references point to the future at the end of the age. In the present New Covenant Era, the Lord is relating to humanity in grace, love, forgiveness, mercy and restoration.

Revelation 16:21

a) Here is a parallel to the plague of hail on Egypt in Exodus 9:18-26. We also see a parallel in Joshua 10:11 when the Lord hurled large hailstones on the Amorites to defeat them. The thought here is that God will completely defeat His enemies and the enemies of His people.

b) Josephus gives us an interesting account of huge stones being hurled on Jerusalem: "The stone missiles weighed a talent and traveled two furlongs or more, and their impact not only on those who were hit first, but also on those behind them, was enormous. At first the Jews kept watch for the stone – for it was white – and its approach was intimated to the eye by its shining surface as well as to the ear by its whizzing sound. Watchmen posted on the towers gave the warnings whenever the engine was fired and the stone came hurtling toward them, shouting in their native tongue: 'The Son is coming!' Those in the line of fire made way and fell prone, a precaution that resulted in the stone's passing harmlessly through and falling in their rear. To frustrate this, it occurred to the Romans to blacken the stones so that they could not be seen so easily beforehand; then they hit their target and destroyed many with a single shot."

c) They cursed God because of the PLEGE – Greek – wound, blow, stripe, not plague in the sense of a disease. Cursing the Almighty is useless and reveals the hardness of heart of those who have determined to resist His LOVE.

CHAPTER SEVENTEEN

As we begin Revelation Chapter Seventeen, we see a contrast of two brides. The False Bride and the True Bride of Christ are contrasted as one being a harlot, and the other a virgin: The Bride of Babylon vs. the Bride of Christ.

This is such an exciting section of Scripture because of all the awesome spiritual symbolism that we will begin to unpack. As we move through this chapter, we will be reminded of spiritual symbolism and allegory which has been explained in detail previously in earlier chapters. We will use these interpretations as a foundation to understand Revelation Seventeen.

This chapter introduces us to the Woman on the Beast and interprets her identity to us as the Roman Empire based upon internal evidence found within the text. Since we have already established our hermeneutic for interpreting Revelation, we will begin our study of the contrast of the two brides: 1) The false/adulterous bride embodied in the Roman Empire, and the people in agreement with that world system; 2) The True Bride of Christ – as described in Revelation 19 – who agrees with her King of Kings and Lord of Lords.

As we conclude Chapter 17, we will read through the angelic interpretations of verses 1-6. We will look at the imagery which contrasts the Harlot/False Bride who agrees with the spirit of animating evil in the world (Satan) to the true Bride who is the Church of Jesus Christ, the shining, pure and white one who is faithful.

For an excellent alternative to my exegesis of Revelation Chapter 17, see Dr. Kenneth Gentry's, *The Divorce of Israel.* This is a wonderful treatment of this section of verses. It is important to note that not all Partial Preterist, Post-Millennial commentators agree uniformly. However, I want to point the reader to other excellent works of scholarship from a Partial Preterist, Post-Millennial view.

Revelation 17:1

a) Verse 1 begins with John having a dialogue with one of the seven angels who is about to speak to John in figurative and symbolic language about the identity of the Woman and the Beast. Later in Revelation 17:7, this same angel begins the interpretation of the symbolism from verses 1-6. Chapter 17 is an easy section of Scripture to interpret because it interprets itself once the identity of the Woman and the Beast has been identified.

b) The angel is showing John the "judgment" of the great prostitute who sits on many waters. The Greek word for judgment is KRIMA – a decree, judgments, condemnation of wrong, the decision (whether severe or mild) which one passes on the faults of others, the sentence of a judge. We see the angel is showing John the reason for judgment through the use of spiritual symbolism that communicates vast amounts of information through that particular symbolism. To understand Revelation is to understand the symbolism contained in the book.

c) Great Prostitute – Greek – MEGAS PORNE – a woman who sells her body for sexual uses, metaphor - an idolatress, of "Babylon" i.e. Rome, the chief seat of idolatry (Strong's) – The identity of the Great Prostitute is easily understood as Rome. In Revelation 13, we looked at these concepts in detail. We see in Scripture that any nation that does not worship God, but instead worships idols is considered to be in spiritual adultery. Israel was in spiritual adultery in many seasons of her history. Ezekiel, Jeremiah and Hosea use this type of symbolism to record those eras. At the time of writing of the Revelation, Rome was engaged in the worst type of spiritual adultery which was the worship of a man, the Caesar of Rome.

d) Many waters – Many times in Scripture, waters are described as the mass of people groups. Rome at this time governed the whole the civilized world. Since we studied this in great detail in Revelation 13, we will not expound on the exegesis of this same symbolism here. *(See Isaiah 17:12 & Isaiah 57:20)*

Revelation 17:2

a) The spiritual symbolism continues in verse 2 where we are given the description of the wide influence of spiritual adultery that Rome exerted on the ancient world. Whenever Rome conquered an area, they introduced Roman culture, Roman currency, the Greco-Roman Pantheon, and Emperor worship into the culture of that conquered territory. Given the massive influence of Rome ruling all of Europe, including the British Isles, Asia Minor, the Middle East and North Africa, Rome definitely caused the kings of the earth to commit adultery. Even Jerusalem was involved in this spiritual adultery when their leadership declared their allegiance to Caesar, and not to Jesus in John 19:12, 15.

b) Being spiritually blinded by idolatry is described as drunkenness/ intoxication. It is a spiritually delusional state to be caught in deception and under the influence of any other spirit than the Holy Spirit. All truth leads to clarity of mind as those who have the Holy Spirit are promised a Spirit of courage and a sound mind. *(See 2 Timothy 1:7)*

c) Wine is the Biblical type and shadow for being under the influence of spiritual deception or judgment. The wine of her adulteries and her committing acts of adultery use the Greek words relating to PORNEO in this verse. A verb and a noun are used in this context. We see the active pursuit of deception, lies, immorality, resulting in the state of being influenced by them.

Revelation 17:3

a) It must have been a vivid and wild experience for John to be in a vision and then suddenly be transported to another spiritual realm within that vision. This is a reminder that it is error to read Revelation with a literalist hermeneutic.

b) We were previously introduced to this Beast in Revelation 13. Let's walk through the symbolism, as this will help us in our interpretation of verse 3.

c) The vision takes place in a desert or deserted place – This is symbolic language for the spiritual waste land where the enemy dwells. Greek – EREMOS – solitary, lonely, desolate, uninhabited, deprived of the aid and protection of others, especially of friends, acquaintances, kindred, of a woman neglected by her husband, from whom the husband withholds himself, of a flock deserted by its shepherd – We see a False Bride here embodied by those who have joined themselves to one who has no love, concern or care.

d) Woman sitting – Greek GYNE KATHEMAI – Verb – to have a fixed abode, to dwell, to sit down, seat one's self.

e) Scarlet Beast – This symbolism is easily interpreted as the generic beast of Revelation 13 (the Roman Empire) being under the influence of the devil/Satan.

f) The seven heads are interpreted for us in Revelation 17:9. This is Rome, the city on seven hills.

g) Ten horns are speaking about many Roman Provinces of that time period. It is important for us to reference Daniel 2:42-45. In the time Jesus was born, Augustus Caesar divided the Roman Empire into ten provinces (toes), and Jesus is the Rock cut without hands that smashed the ten toes. His kingdom through the ages will have dominion in increasing measure until His glorious return.

h) The blasphemous names speak of all of the blasphemies of idol worship, Emperor worship, sexual immorality, unjust economies, slave trading and cultural degradation of the Roman Empire. What is awesome is that in the first three centuries of the Church of Jesus Christ, she converted the Woman who sits on the Beast! The True Bride conquered the False Bride!

Revelation 17:4-5

a) Dressed in purple – This color is reserved for royalty and the rich. We see a false or counterfeit identity of this unfaithful woman contrasted to the True Bride of Christ who is a royal princess arrayed in White!

b) Scarlet – Red can speak of anger, passion, or redemption. This false bride/adulterous woman is inflamed with the ungodly passions of the spirit that animates this beast.

c) Glittering with gold – False glory

d) Precious stones – Gem stones speak of wealth and riches. Gem stones are used as descriptive language of the One who sat on the throne in Revelation 4. The tribes of Israel were represented by gem stones on the breast plate of the High Priest as a symbol of being close to the Lord's heart. This woman is arrayed in false wealth and riches, and is not a gem carried close to the Lord's heart. She has no covenant.

e) Pearls are used in the context of wisdom and as a descriptive for the kingdom of God in Scripture. *(See Job 28:18 & Matthew 13)* This woman has no wisdom or enduring kingdom from God.

f) Her cup is filth – A cup speaks of destiny. Jesus referred to His destiny as having a cup given to Him by the Father to become the Lamb of God. Cups also speak of fellowship in Scripture.

Psalm 116:12 speaks of fellowship with God as the cup of salvation. This symbolism proves this woman has false fellowship and a destiny full of destruction.

g) Her title tells the whole story – Rome is the embodiment of everything contrary to the goodness of God.

Revelation 17:6

a) Verse 6 tells us the woman persecuted the Bride of Christ to the point where she was drunk with their blood. This would have been very welcome news to the First Century Church who suffered immensely under her rule.

b) To summarize, this woman was defeated by the decree of the Lord Jesus and the power evangelism of the Early Church. This would have seemed an impossibility to the Apostolic Church who received the Revelation of John. If they looked at the power of Rome, its massive military, economic strength, and wide spread idolatry and immorality, they could have easily been discouraged. However, they chose to believe in their identity as God's very own. They believed His decree of judgment on Rome, and lived in fidelity to Him. The Church is responsible for the continuing defeat of this spirit of adultery in every age.

Revelation 17:7

a) John was greatly astonished by the vision of the Woman on the Beast. The Greek word for astonish or wonder is THAUMAZ – to wonder, wonder at, marvel, to be wondered at, to be held in admiration. This speaks of the alluring deception of the power of the world, the deception of luxury, and the plastic beauty of societies who love decadence. It can seem impossible for the Bride of Christ to overcome these social structures' power, but we know that greater is He who is in us than he who is in the world. It our birthright to overcome and influence the world for God's greater glory. He is the legal possessor of all things.

b) The angel re-directs John's gaze and explains the mystery of the alluring vision he just witnessed. The interpretation of Revelation 17 is given to us by the angel who will explain the symbolism of the woman, the beast, the heads and the ten horns.

Revelation 17:8

a) We have two movements in verse 8. The first movement is regarding the destiny of the beast, which is destruction. The second movement is regarding the sure destruction of those who partner with the beast.

b) We must refer to Revelation 13:3 when we consider verse 8. Revelation 13:3 tells us that one of the heads of the beast suffered what appeared to be a mortal wound, and yet was healed and the world was astonished by this. This refers to the following political occurrences at that time.

c) Rome is easily identified as the beast. The Roman Emperor, Nero, committed suicide at the height of Roman dominance and power. When Nero committed suicide, the Julian Dynasty was suddenly ended, as Nero had no offspring or bloodline heir to the throne. He had murdered all familial opponents to his rule. It is important to mention that it was a common name to refer to Nero as a Beast by the Roman Senate and others in Roman culture. Therefore, it could be said that the Generic Beast (Rome) had suffered a fatal wound to its head.

d) At that time, the Roman Empire went into a short period of political civil wars, and wars of rebellion that plunged the Empire into deep political upheaval. Vespasian was able to realign allegiances and put down rebellion to restore/revive the beast with the fatal wound. The Roman Empire was resurrected and the Flavian Dynasty was established. Basically, the Beast came out of the pit/abyss.

e) The second movement is regarding those who joined

themselves to the harlot. It is sure death to live for any system than the system of Life found in the Kingdom of God.

f) When we look at the language "from the creation of the world," some say eternal destiny is predetermined. This is simply not the case. I cannot accept a loving God would appoint a portion of His creation, made in His image, to an eternal hell. This phrase is easily understood when one looks at it in the context of God's omniscience. As God is transcendent, outside of time and space, He knows beginning from end, but does not control the outcomes of those who chose either to love Him or live in their Adamic rebellion.

g) Most assuredly, when Vespasian consolidated power and revived Rome's power and authority, the people of the land, especially those in the Jewish rebellion against Rome were amazed. A good knowledge of the history and the context of the Scriptures we are reading keeps us safe from speculative doctrines that draw conclusions from Scripture which are completely outside of the people and the culture they were written to. We can be sure these verses declaring the fall of Rome would have been good news for the Apostle John who was being exiled by the Beast of Rome.

Revelation 17:9

a) The mind of wisdom - Mind - Greek - NOUS - the mind, comprising alike the faculties of perceiving and understanding and those of feeling, judging, determining.

b) Wisdom - Greek - SOPHIA - wisdom, broad and full of intelligence; used of the knowledge of very diverse matters.

c) What is being communicated here is that when one looks at these prophetic symbols, one can understand. The First Century Christians of the Seven Churches would have been able to interpret these symbols. We also have the witness of the whole of Church History that uniformly agreed to the earliest interpretation of these symbols until the 1860's.

d) The city on seven hills is easily identified as Rome by a simple knowledge of the geography of the city of Rome. They were Aventinus, Caelius, Esquilinus, Palantinus, Quirinalis, Caitolinus, and Viminalis.

Revelation 17:10-11

a) A list of kings in succession who are going to destruction. The first five Kings/Caesars were Julius, Augustus, Tiberius, Caligula, and Claudius.

b) The one is Nero.

c) Galba is the seventh King/Caesar. He reigned for less than seven months and was murdered by the Military Commander, Otho.

d) The eighth King/Caesar is understood to be the animating spirit behind the antichrist political system of the Roman Caesars until her fall (Constantine). The text itself: "The beast which was and is not (Rome), is himself also an eighth and is one (of the same type – Greek – EK – out of, from, by, away from) of the seven, and he goes to destruction."

e) To quote scholar David Chilton for clarity: "But the fall of the Julio-Claudian dynasty and the severe political chaos attending it must not be interpreted by Christians to mean the end of troubles. For their real enemy is **the Beast**, who will become incarnated in other Caesars as well. He is also **an eighth king**, yet is of the seven: the anti-christian brutality of succeeding tyrants will mark them as being of the same stripe as their predecessors. Eight is the number of resurrection in the Bible; St. John is warning that even though the Empire will seem to disintegrate after the rule of the seven kings, it will be "resurrected" again, to live on in other persecutors of the Church.

Yet the Empire's comeback will not result in victory for the Beast, for even the eighth, the resurrected Beast, **goes to destruction**. The Church will have to exercise patience during the period of the Beast's ascendancy, but she has the assurance that her enemies will not succeed. Their King will be victorious; His servants have been predestined to share in His triumph."

f) The good news is that we are NOT looking forward to a modern revived Roman Empire who will begin to persecute Christians and cause hell on earth. We have already defeated this Beast by the power of our Gospel thousands of years ago.

Revelation 17:12

a) It is common knowledge the Roman Empire had provinces ruled by vassal kings. These vassal kings pledged allegiance to Rome and the persecutions of Christians was Empire wide.

Revelation 17:13-14

a) It is a manifestation of all political entities to wage war against the rule of God. *(See Psalm 2)*

b) It is also the ultimate goal of those who choose a reprobate mind to war against everything that is godly. This struggle has been from the foundation of the world. From Cain against Abel, to Nimrod and every other world leader or common culture who has rejected the witness of creation which points us to God. *(See Romans 1:18-20)*

c) Philippians 2 teaches us the same theme found in Revelation 17:13-14. This would have been very encouraging to the early church living in the midst of this tribulation.

d) Ignatius of Antioch said: "May I enjoy the wild beasts that are prepared for me. I pray that they would be found eager to rush at me, and I will also entice them to devour me speedily and not deal with me as some, whom out of fear they have not touched. If they are unwilling to assail me, I will compel them to do so. Pardon me; I know what is to my benefit. Now I begin to be a disciple. Let no one, of things visible or invisible, prevent me from attaining to Jesus Christ. Let fire and the cross; let wild beasts; let tearings, breakings, and dislocation of bones; let cutting off of limbs; let shatterings of the whole body; and let all the evil torments of the devil come upon me; only let me attain to Jesus Christ."

Revelation 17:15-18

a) The waters are all the people groups the Roman Empire ruled. The woman is the spirit of Babylon/Mystery Babylon that has influenced all world powers in every era of history.

b) The woman will be humiliated by the Scriptural symbols listed.

c) Naked – To be humiliated and uncovered. *(See Isaiah 47:2-3, Jeremiah 13:26, Ezekiel 16:37, Hosea 2:10)*

d) Eat her flesh – We can reference the demise of Jezebel whose flesh was eaten by dogs in 2 Kings 9:30-37. Just as Rome persecuted the prophetic voice of the Church, the spirit of Jezebel always seeks to silence prophets of God.

e) Burn her with fire *(See Jeremiah 4:11-13, 30-31, Ezekiel 16:37-41)*

f) Rome and Jerusalem, who were both spiritual adulterers, were both burned to the ground.

g) The great city who rules over the earth is easily interpreted as the Roman Empire. Rome ruled the most territory of any empire ever in world history.

Summary

As we conclude Revelation 17, we can see that not only was the Roman Empire destroyed by her political enemies and the propagation of

Christianity, so also Jerusalem was destroyed by her rejection of Jesus and the New Covenant He offered. All empires, nations and systems will suffer the same fate at the return of Jesus Christ. Spiritually, by the conquest of the Church as she preaches the Gospel of love, and in fullness when Jesus overthrows all systems at His return.

CHAPTER EIGHTEEN

As Revelation Chapter Seventeen introduced us to the identity of the Mystery Babylon – the Mother of Prostitutes – which is Rome/Roman Empire that is animated with the spiritual realms of darkness and the dragon/devil, Revelation Chapter Eighteen shows us the destruction of the Roman Empire from heaven's perspective and details the spiritual warfare surrounding her fall. Revelation 17 was a wide view of the political system of Rome from the perspective of the spiritual realm; Revelation 18 is the judgment and the indictment of Rome from heaven's perspective. In it, we see the angelic order announcing its destruction and the reasons for its destruction.

As we look at the real history of the Roman Empire, we can easily see the fulfillment of the prophesied destruction of Rome in precise detail as prophesied by John.

We also see in Revelation 18 the destruction of the spirit of Babylon in every age during the Church/Grace Age. Just as the Roman Empire was destroyed for agreeing with the dominion of the beast and the shedding of the blood of the saints, all empires and tyrannies of men that oppress God's people and shed their blood, are under the same indictment.

Revelation 18:1-3

a) Verse 1 introduces us to an angel of MEGAS EXOUSIA who was coming down from heaven, the dwelling place of God. Revelation is fascinating in that we see the diversity of the angelic order in all their assignments and ministries in the heavens. This particular angel was given great authority – EXOUSIA – the power of choice, the power to judge, the power to do as one pleases, royal authority – this shows us that this particular angel's ministry was to decree and put into action the judgment of Babylon the Great, which is Rome.

b) In Chapter 17, we were given the identity of Mystery Babylon and the wide overview of her pending destruction. In Revelation 18 , we get to see the specific judgment decree and the reasons for her judgment from heaven's perspective.

c) It is interesting that it took centuries for the whole judgment to come into view. This shows us that these judgments against Rome/Roman Empire were part of a process that allowed the Church to participate in the judgment as She evangelized and overthrew the religious pagan Roman cults by the Gospel. Lastly, the animating spirit behind the spiritual adultery of Rome is still in the world, and even now the Church of Jesus Christ is gaining ground with victory as the centuries have passed. Eventually at the return of Jesus Christ, the animating spirit of rebellion (the devil/dragon) will be completely defeated.

d) As previously mentioned, Babylon was synonymous with Rome. *(See 1 Peter 5:13 & Revelation 17:9)* The Early Church referred to Rome as Babylon because of the similarities of the historical Babylon and its dealings with Israel. Tertullian was one of the Early Church Fathers who held that position. Now that we have established the identity of Mystery Babylon as Rome, verse 2 begins to outline the judgment.

e) Rome had become a haunt for demons. The Greek word is KATOIKETERION – which means an abode or a habitation. The NIV translation is lacking as the second part of verse 2 says that Babylon has also become a Prison – Greek – PHYLAKE – of the place where captives are kept, a prison, and held under watch. Birds are also considered as symbolic of demonic activity and influence.

f) Ancient Roman society was so degenerate as the demonic realm had embedded itself so deeply into it that was judged by the Lord. In the same way, the world systems of every generation are influenced and often in agreement with demonic values and thoughts. This introduces us to two theological concepts: 1) Jesus calls the Church salt and light. One of our primary missions is to preserve society by mixing into it and influencing it by godly living, etc. In ancient times, salt was a used a preservative for meat. 2) Light dispels darkness. As Jesus Christ becomes manifest in our lives, we displace darkness by our kingdom authority, spiritual gifts and the wisdom of God operating in us. This has a redemptive effect on the nations of the world. Much of our spiritual warfare is waged in the practical things that we do every day.

g) The nations that were ruled by Rome embraced her religion, government and economic system in that they engaged in the spiritual adultery of Emperor Worship, pagan cultism, and the luxuries of excess.

h) Proverbs 15:6 – Great wealth is in the house of the righteous, But trouble is in the income of the wicked. – There is a difference between the economies of God and the unjust economies of the world systems. The economies of God run on generosity, justice, and righteousness. The economies of the world systems run on tyranny, injustice and inequality.

Revelation 18:4-6

a) We are reminded of Isaiah 52:11 – Depart, depart, go out from there! Touch no unclean thing! Come out from it and be pure, you who carry the articles of the LORD's house. – This verse is a charge to the Levites/Priesthood to not engage themselves in the sin that was in the land at that time. As the Church of Jesus

Christ, we are a royal priesthood (1 Peter 2:9), and the Church in the First Century was being warned by this prophesy not to agree with the common culture of their day.

b) It was probably very comforting for the Early Church to hear that they were going to be avenged by the Lord for all the persecutions, murders, humiliations, and imprisonments they had suffered at the hands of the Roman authorities. Rome was going to suffer a double portion for what she did to the Christians in the First Century. On August 24, 410, Rome was sacked and destroyed by the Visigoths led by Alaric I. St. Jerome wrote, "The City which had taken the whole world was itself taken."

Revelation 18:7-8

a) Rome sat as a queen/Jezebel and it is the pride of cultures to build themselves up and expect no consequences for their actions. Proverbs 11:2 – When pride comes, then comes disgrace, but with humility comes wisdom. 1 John 2:16 – For everything in the world—the lust of the flesh, the lust of the eyes, and the pride of life—comes not from the Father but from the world.

b) Alaric I sieged Rome in AD 408 and exacted the following vast amounts of wealth from Rome: The city was forced to give the Goths 5,000 pounds of gold; 30,000 pounds of silver; 4,000 silken tunics; 3,000 hides dyed scarlet; and 3,000 pounds of pepper in exchange for lifting the siege. Later he sieged Rome two more times and ultimately burned it down in 410. We can see clearly in history that Rome fell exactly as it was prophesied.

Revelation 18:9-10

a) It is common historical knowledge that the Roman Empire suffered economic collapse as a result of the sack in 410. The Roman economy was based upon fiat currency which did not have intrinsic value of itself, but was represented by an amount of gold or silver that was endorsed by Rome, much like our dollar and other major currencies of the world today. When Rome was emptied of her riches, the currency was worthless. Many in the Empire would have been mourning the loss of their wealth.

Revelation 18:11-13

a) In Verses 11-13, we see a list of the luxuries that were traded throughout the Roman Empire. Rome held vast amounts of regional influence. Riches and wealth from all over the whole civilized world was traded throughout the Empire. We can see this to be true by the diversity of the items on this list.

b) The most disturbing item on this list is the bodies and the souls of men. The estimation of the population of slavery in the First Century was 30-50%. There is no precise demography for Ancient Rome, but these are the best estimates.

c) We see our God Almighty detests slavery and judged Rome for it. People are made in God's image while slavery defaces and devalues God's very own creation.

d) It is also disturbing to see that Rome somehow trafficked in the souls of men. This may refer to the influence of Emperor Worship, paganism and demon worship which was rampant in common Roman culture. It may also refer to the corrupting influence of the spirit of disobedience and rebellion inspired by the dragon. Whatever it is, we can conclude it is alarming that souls of men can be trafficked by world systems.

e) As the Church, we are charged with the reformation of society. The Mystery Babylon was overthrown by the Early Church and the Church had Christianized the whole of Europe by the Middle Ages. We are encouraged in Scripture to not only engage this warfare of influence for the nations of world by the Gospel of Love, but to transcend it in Love, expanding the influence of the Kingdom in every age.

Revelation 18:14-15

a) As we continue hearing the lament of the merchant class in the Roman Empire over the fall of Mystery Babylon/Rome in verse 14, we see that the world system of that time and of today longs for fruit that is contrary to the fruit of Spirit and the treasures of the Kingdom of heaven. Riches and splendor are cheap plastic compared to the knowledge of God and a life centered on Him. The merchant class wept because of their lives were based on temporal pleasures and a false reality. Their wealth was gained by agreeing with a corrupt economy.

b) Mark 8:35-36 – For whoever wishes to save his life will lose it, but whoever loses his life for My sake and the gospel's will save it. For what does it profit a man to gain the whole world, and forfeit his soul?

c) We will receive the fruit of whatever system or dominion we choose to live in.

d) Contrasted to the destruction of the Roman Empire and the spirit of Babylon which continues today, Christians belong to a Kingdom "where no thief comes near nor moth destroys." Not only do we walk in present day promises now, we possess eternal wealth.

e) The fruit of the Spirit contrasted to the fruit of the world/sinful nature. *(See Galatians 6:18-23)* As believers we have a distinct advantage in terms of life skills, quality of life and what we present to the world. If we are not manifesting the fruit of Spirit or the witness of the Spirit, we need to ask for more of the Spirit. We can never accomplish Christ-like living on our own. It is a grace given to us by Holy Spirit.

Revelation 18:16-17

a) Verses 16-17 take us back to Revelation 17:3-4 and the contrast of this woman, who is a false bride when compared to the True

Bride, the collective Church of Jesus Christ. Dressed in purple – This color is reserved for royalty and the rich. We see a false, or counterfeit, identity of this unfaithful woman contrasted to the True Bride of Christ who is a royal princess arrayed in White!

b) Scarlet – Red can either speak of anger, passion, or redemption. This false bride/adulterous woman is inflamed with the ungodly passions of the spirit that animates this beast.

c) Glittering with gold – False glory.

d) Precious stones – Gem stones speak of wealth and riches. Gem stones are used as descriptive language of the One who sat on the throne in Revelation 4. Also, the tribes of Israel were represented by gem stones on the breast plate of the High Priest as a symbol being close to the Lord's heart. This woman is arrayed in false wealth and riches, and is not a gem carried close to the Lord's heart. She has no covenant.

e) Pearls are used in the context of wisdom and as a descriptive for the Kingdom of God in Scripture. *(See Job 28:18 & Matthew 13)* This woman has no wisdom or an enduring kingdom from God.

f) Her cup is filth. Cups speak of destinies: Jesus referred to His destiny as a cup being given to Him by the Father to become the sacrificed Lamb of God. Cups also speak of fellowship in Scripture, as well. Psalm 116:12 speaks of fellowship with God as the cup of salvation. What we see here in the symbolism is that this woman has false fellowship and a destiny of destruction.

g) Her title "Mystery Babylon, Mother of Prostitutes" tells the whole story. Rome is the embodiment of everything contrary to the goodness of God.

Revelation 18:17-20

a) In the previous verses, we looked at the destruction of Rome in history by Alaric I in AD 410. In verses 17-19, we see this destruction in apocalyptic symbolism and language that is found throughout the Old Testament Scriptures.

b) It is important to keep in view that we are hearing "another voice" from heaven, so the things we are reading are from heaven's perspective.

c) Verse 20 would have been particularly hopeful and encouraging for the First Century Christians who were reading or hearing the Revelation read to them in their churches. The church of the early Roman era suffered tremendously. The Lord took vengeance upon Rome because of her persecution of apostles, prophets and faithful saints, and for her allegiance to the beast, as symbolized by the woman riding the dragon.

d) The Roman Historian Tacitus gives us the first non-Christian mention of our faith in secular history in AD 64: "Yet no human effort, no princely largess nor offerings to the gods could make that infamous rumor disappear that Nero had somehow ordered the fire. Therefore, in order to abolish that rumor, Nero falsely accused and executed with the most exquisite punishments those people called Christians, who were infamous for their abominations. The originator of the name, Christ, was executed as a criminal by the procurator Pontius Pilate during the reign of Tiberius; and though repressed, this destructive superstition erupted again, not only through Judea, which was the origin of this evil, but also through the city of Rome, to which all that is horrible and shameful floods together and is celebrated. Therefore, first those were seized who admitted their faith, and then, using the information they provided, a vast multitude were convicted, not so much for the crime of burning the city, but for hatred of the human race. And perishing they were additionally made into sports: they were killed by dogs by having the hides of beasts attached to them, or they were nailed to crosses or set aflame, and, when the daylight passed away, they were used as nighttime lamps. Nero gave his own gardens for this spectacle and performed a Circus game, in the habit of a charioteer mixing with the plebs or driving about the race-course. Even though they were clearly guilty and merited being made the most recent example of the consequences of crime, people began to pity these sufferers, because they were consumed not for the public good but on account of the fierceness of one man (Nero)."

Revelation 18:21-24

a) Verses 21-24 introduce us to a Mighty Angel who is charged with an action in the spiritual realm that will manifest in the natural realm in the destruction of the Roman Empire and the city of Rome in particular. This angel's judgment declaration is from the Lord. Verses 21-14 show us the spiritual warfare that surrounded the spread of the gospel into ancient Rome, and the victory of God's kingdom over the inferior dominion of the beast/devil.

b) It is important for us to keep in mind that we are always warring for the destiny of our planet from a place of sure victory. Revelation reveals that truth to us as we seek reformation in our own nation.

c) The millstone is a symbol of the defeat of destruction in the Scriptures. *(See Deut. 6:24, Judges 9:53, 2 Samuel 11:21 & Mark 18:6)*

d) The sea here is symbolic of the mass of humanity under the Roman Empire. The angel in the spirit realm warred against the demonic forces empowering Babylon/Rome by this spiritual act and declaration.

e) Every system of Roman culture and society were affected by this decisive angelic action. In verse 22 arts and entertainment, manufacturing, agriculture, wisdom/education, family, and religion were all condemned as corrupt because of their rejection of the Gospel and their persecution of the Church.

f) The Spirit-filled and Christ-like Church is aligned with the right Kingdom. It possesses better wisdom and better systems of living than the corrupt systems that are aligned with the beast.

g) Verse 24 points us to the truth that righteous bloodshed will always be accounted for. Just as Jerusalem was held accountable for all the blood of the prophets, especially the blood of Jesus (Matthew 23:35-36), Rome was responsible for her persecutions of Christians and their righteous bloodshed. Lastly, even today as the Church is being persecuted throughout the Middle East and Asia, all will be held accountable.

Galatians 6:7-8 – "Do not be deceived, God is not mocked; for whatever a man sows, this he will also reap. For the one who sows to his own flesh will from the flesh reap corruption, but the one who sows to the Spirit will from the Spirit reap eternal life."

CHAPTER NINETEEN

In Revelation Chapter Nineteen, we are wooed by the Holy Spirit into the revelation of the glory of God for His Church as we gaze upon His salvation narrative. As we do this, I am sure we will be captivated by His love for the Bride, His Church.

Revelation 19 begins with a five-section heavenly antiphonal worship song that will direct our hearts into the faithfulness of God to His Bride.

As Revelation 18 was the indictment of the unfaithful prostitute of the world system (specifically Rome and apostate Jerusalem we found in Revelation 16), we see in Revelation 19 the fidelity and honor of the Bride of Christ, the Church. Revelation 19 completes the contrast of the two women: the spiritually adulterous Woman riding the Beast, and the pure and spotless Bride of Christ, the Church.

Revelation 19 also shows us the wide view of the authority, and power of Jesus Christ as a conquering King and exalted Messiah, the King of Kings and Lord of Lords. We see the Church following the leadership of Jesus bringing the His Kingdom to the nations of the world.

Revelation 19:11-21 gives us the most majestic, powerful and authoritative view of Jesus Christ in the Scriptures. These verses present to us the highest Christology found in Scripture. In fact, I believe that a season of prayer and meditation on these verses will bring a transformation of the way we personally view Jesus Christ spiritually and how we think about Him.

What we believe about God colors our lives in every area. Having the highest view of Jesus releases truth, perseverance, faith, breakthrough and miracles into our lives and the lives of others. We can only re-image Jesus accurately as His representatives on earth by growing in our personal experiential knowledge of Him.

As we begin this chapter, I want us to set our hearts on Jesus, the Rider on the White Horse, and ask the Holy Spirit to bring us revelation and illumination as we go verse-by-verse gazing upon the glory of our Savior.

Revelation 19:1

a) As the great multitude in heaven witnessed the destruction of the Adulterous Woman/World System of Rome, they praised the Lord for His righteous judgments. This multitude was most likely made up of believers in heaven and the angelic assemblies. The sound in the spirit realm that John was witnessing must have been an amazing experience. One can only imagine the volume and reverberations of their voices praising God.

b) It is interesting to note that the only uses of the original word *Hallelujah* in the New Testament are used in Revelation 19. They are used four times in connection to the defeat of the adulterous world system and the re-conquest of the earth by Jesus and His Church.

c) Three truths about God are highlighted to us in verse 1. Salvation – SOTERIA – Greek – deliverance, preservation, safety, salvation, deliverance from the molestation of enemies, future salvation, the sum of benefits and blessings which the Christians, redeemed from all earthly ills, will enjoy after the visible Return of Christ from heaven in the consummated and eternal Kingdom of God – Only through Jesus Christ can our whole person be saved, kept and delivered to eternity. This is a work of God, not man. This truth keeps us from the spirit of religion which robs God of glory by denying this truth.

d) Glory – Greek – DOXA – good opinion concerning one, resulting in praise, honor, and glory, splendor, brightness, magnificence, excellence, preeminence, dignity, grace – All goodness belongs to the Godhead. He is true and worthy to place trust in Him. The Early Church needed to be convinced of His goodness and His promises, otherwise, they would have never prevailed against the Beast of Rome or the persecution of the unbelieving Jews who denied Jesus was Messiah.

e) Power – Greek – DYNAMIS – strength, power, ability, inherent power, power residing in a thing by virtue of its nature, or which a person or thing exerts and puts forth, power for performing miracles, moral power and excellence of soul, the power and influence which belong to riches and wealth, power consisting in or resting upon armies, forces, hosts.

f) Salvation, glory and power belong to God alone. These declarations of worship point us to the truth that the Lord can be completely trusted for all things in life.

Revelation 19:2

a) True and just are His judgments – The judgments of God on the great prostitute, or MEGAS PORNE in the Greek, reveal to us the righteousness of God. We tend to think of judgment as a very negative thing. In reality, it is negative when humans are involved. However, God – being completely un-defiled, pure and possessing all knowledge – makes perfect judgments.

b) At this point, it is important to be reminded that Revelation is a prophecy. 1 Corinthians 14:3 – But one who prophesies speaks to men for edification, exhortation and consolation (for strengthening, encouragement and comfort). Revelation would have been a tremendous comfort to the believers in the First Century through the Third Century as they experienced the Great Tribulation. *(See Revelation 1:1-3)*

c) The Lord had avenged the blood of His servants. Servants – Greek – DOULOS – servants, bond-servants, devoted to another to the disregard of one's own interests. Those who, as an act of their will, join themselves to the purposes of Christ will be defended, and avenged. The number of martyrs in the Roman Colosseum in Rome was estimated at 500,000. There is no way to corroborate this as a hard number, but anthropologists have found no shortage of skeletons from that era. Church History also documents thousands of Christians were martyred in that era. In Revelation 6:9-10, the martyrs asked, "how long will it be before you avenge our blood?"

d) The first verse of this antiphonal worship song is comprised of verses 1-2.

Revelation 19:3

a) Verse 3 starts the second verse of this worship song. It begins with the glorious hallelujah declaration of the believers and angels in heaven.

b) The smoke goes up forever and ever. This is Old Testament speech that communicates the finality of the judgment. We would reference Genesis 19 in the destruction of Sodom and Gomorrah and Isaiah 34:10, where it prophesies that the smoke of Babylon's destruction would rise forever.

c) Isaiah 34:10 – It will not be quenched night or day; Its smoke will go up forever. From generation to generation it will be desolate; None will pass through it forever and ever.

Revelation 19:4

a) John sees into the Throne Room of heaven with the 24 Elders and Four Living Creatures worshiping God, giving their overwhelming approval on the judgment of Rome, Jerusalem, and (ultimately) the entire world system. *Amen* is the word of strong agreement, or may it be done, or this word is firm and faithful.

This is the third verse of the 5-Fold antiphonal worship song of believers, angels, elders and creatures singing back and forth in heaven.

b) It is important to point out the fluidity of this vision: In one verse John is one place and then suddenly in the next he is in another spiritual place. It is serious error to read Revelation chrono-logically. It is best understood by allowing the Scriptures to interpret Scripture. Many of the themes and ideas were already given to us the Old Testament apocalyptic books of Isaiah, Jeremiah, Lamentations, Ezekiel, Daniel and the Minor Prophets. These themes self-interpret Revelation.

Revelation 19:5

a) The voice from the Throne is understood as the voice of Jesus encouraging His people to praise Him and the works of the Father. John 20:17 – But go to My brethren and say to them, 'I ascend to My Father and your Father, and My God and your God.'

b) Those who fear God great and small – Greek – PHOBEO – to reverence, venerate, to treat with deference or reverential obedience – The fear of God is not fearing He will do harm to us. It is recognizing the love, grace, goodness, glory, power and majesty of God as we willingly and lovingly submit to Him. He is perfect in all His ways, and His ways will do us no harm. Jesus, being the perfect representation of the Father, showed us what His leadership looks like.

c) This is the fourth verse of this antiphonal/worship song/liturgy in heaven.

Revelation 19:6

a) As we come to the last chorus of this song, the volume increases because Jesus had encouraged the worship into a crescendo. It is a three-fold increase: Voices, waters and thunders!

b) Three – The number of resurrection, newness of life, divinity and power. It is a common number found throughout Revelation.

c) As the last chorus begins, it begins with high praise and worshipful declarations! Our God reigns! He is glorious, and we take pleasure in who He is!

Revelation 19:7

a) The "Wedding Day of the Lamb has come" has been understood two different ways in Church History.

b) The first understanding is that the Harlot Jerusalem has been divorced, and the marriage of the Church to Her Husband, Jesus, has been consummated by His suffering on the cross, His resurrection, and finally the outpouring of the Holy Spirit at Pentecost where the Church became the True Bride of God. This is confirmed in the New Testament. *(See Ephesians 5:25-27 & 2 Corinthians 11:2-3)*

c) The second understanding is that we are seeing a very wide panoramic view of the whole of Church history culminating in the Return of Jesus Christ as the Bridegroom, and the Church coming into her fullness as a Bride. I mention both because I believe we need to be intellectually honest in our interpretation of Scripture, due to the statement "the bride has made herself ready."

d) We must ask the following rhetorical questions: Is the Church a Bride now? Has each one of us made ourselves ready to be joined to Him? Will there be a generation of believers that will finally live in the place of identity and fidelity to the point where Jesus returns because she is ready?

Revelation 19:8

a) The Bride is clothed in fine linen, clean and bright. The Greek words suggest more than our English words indicate. The fine linen indicates that this is a very fine raiment, exquisitely made of the best material. The word clean means purified by fire, pruned, free from corruption and sin, free from the mixture of dissimilar materials, and physically clean. The word bright means transparent and shining.

b) Our righteous acts, or acts of service, is the transparent beautiful covering that reflects His true nature and character. We are covered by Jesus' blood which has washed us and made us clean before God. This is where faith and action kiss, and we act like our Father and our Teacher, Jesus. In fact, the Holy Spirit helps us by being the guiding internal voice of every believer in Jesus, to act according to our identity.

Revelation 19:9

a) The angel confirms the vision John has just witnessed in heaven is true. This would confirm that those who received this prophecy in the Seven Churches mentioned in the beginning of the book could trust the vision and take courage they are not being misled.

b) Blessed are those who are invited! This takes us to Jesus' parable of the wedding to the Pharisees in Matthew 22. In the parable, the King (God), invites His people to celebrate the wedding of His Son. They all have excuses why they cannot come. Then the King declares they did not deserve to come, so He sent servants out all over to fill the banquet hall with anyone who would come.

c) The invitation still stands today. All who would receive the invitation to the wedding will be accepted.

d) God is in a good mood! He loves celebrations and celebrating. God's narrative of salvation history is one of celebrating His relationship with humanity, and reclaiming what was lost in Eden.

e) An interesting note: The Early Church Fathers held that the marriage supper of the Lamb is the Eucharist.

Revelation 19:10

a) Even the Apostle John almost fell into the temptation to worship angels by prostrating himself to this angel. The angel corrects John and directs his attention to bow down to the Lord only.

b) Remarkably, the angel placed himself on the same level as John as one who holds the testimony of Jesus. This shows us that the angelic beings have free will to align their hearts in agreement with God. We also see angels are servants and submitted to the purposes of God. Hebrews tells they are ministering spirits to minister to those being saved. That is us!

c) The testimony of Jesus is the spirit of prophecy. Greek – MARTYRIA IESOUS EIMI PNEUMA PROPHETEIA – The testimony, the office committed to the prophets of testifying concerning future events, as one testifies before a judge, about Jesus, is the spirit, the immaterial essence that animates something, is the divine discourse of declaring the purposes of God.

d) Every time we speak about the salvation narrative of God in Jesus Christ we are declaring God's future to that individual or to the people we are addressing. Numbers 11:19 – But Moses said to him, "Are you jealous for my sake? Would that all the LORD'S people were prophets, that the LORD would put His Spirit upon them!" Today, all believers have the Spirit of God in them, and we are all able to speak under the influence of the Holy Spirit.

Revelation 19:11

a) John sees heaven opened – Everything has been removed from view except the glorious and victorious Lord Jesus Christ. There is nothing that competes with Him as we gaze on Jesus as our Lord and Savior.

b) The White Horse is prophetic symbolism of the strength, power, authority and purity of the Holy One. This horse is a war horse. This clear view of Jesus on the white horse presents Him as conquering King.

c) Faithful and True – Jesus is the only Faithful Witness who represented the heart of the Father in perfection. He was the obedient Son of Man (Adam), who fully obeyed the Father and brought Him pleasure. Jesus said in John 14:9, "Anyone who has seen Me has seen the Father." Philippians 2:6-11 presents Jesus as the faithful and obedient Son who loved the Father so much, He became obedient unto death.

d) Jesus being the Faithful and True One is our source of acceptance for the Father. When we speak of Jesus as faithful and true, we are speaking in terms of Him being trustworthy, the source of truth, the One who worked an obedience we were incapable of. We have been invited to draw from Him and be strengthened from His work. Grace is in full view here when Jesus is called Faithful and True. In the letter to the Laodicean Church, Jesus used this title.

e) With justice/righteousness He makes/wages war – Greek – DIKAIOSYNE – justice/righteousness, integrity, virtue, purity of life, rightness, correctness of thinking feeling, and acting, in a broad sense: state of him who is as he ought to be, righteousness, the condition acceptable to God – When we look at the justice and righteousness of Jesus in regards to Him waging war, our perspective needs to be pointed to the truth that Jesus is conquering and warring against anything that disagrees with the heart of the Father. All injustice, evil, oppression, either spiritual or in the natural realm is the battlefield of this war. Jesus wages war with truth as the Word of God, and uses the Church to advance His heart. This is a war against the demonic realm *(See Ephesians 6:10-18 & 2 Corinthians 10:4)*, and a war of the Love in the natural realm.

f) Revelation 19 is understood in the context of Jesus, with His Church behind Him, going out in the power of the Gospel to conquer spiritual realms of darkness and convert the globe to Christianity by discipling nations. *(See Matthew 28:18-20)*

Revelation 19:12

a) Revelation 19:12 takes us back to the same imagery and symbolism as Revelation 1:13-16.

b) Jesus having blazing eyes speaks of His passion, intensity and zeal for His Church and His cause. Beholding His gaze burns away every lesser love and empowers us to co-labor with Him.

c) On His head are many crowns or diadems – There is no number of crowns listed because Jesus is infinitely powerful and the Only Sovereign. His Kingdom is everlasting and the advance of His Kingdom is never ending.

d) Isaiah 9:7 – There will be no end to the increase of His government or of peace; on the throne of David and over his kingdom, to establish it and to uphold it with justice and righteousness from then on and forevermore. The zeal of the LORD of hosts will accomplish this.

e) Jesus having a Name only He knows points to His divinity as the Second Person of the Holy Trinity. Only God fully knows Himself. To know someone's name in ancient thought is to know them intimately. The mystery of God's Name is the great pursuit of our faith because as God is infinite and self-existent, we will never exhaust exploring the nuances of His NAME.

Revelation 19:13

a) Jesus robe dipped in blood – The Greek word is BAPTO which means immersed. We are pointed to an allegory that communicates two truths: 1) Jesus blood is the defeat of sin and death, as well as the defeat of Satan and his demonic hordes;

2) Jesus blood is the sufficiency and all powerful substance that, when applied, is the answer for all things.

b) Some theologians have presented that this garment is dipped in the blood of Jesus' enemies. I personally do hold that view, because Jesus blood is the substance that conquers sin, defeats the satanic forces, and reforms nations, not the blood of His enemies.

c) His name is the Word of God – This communicates to us that Jesus is eternal. *(See John 1:1-3)* Jesus, the Word of God also communicates that He is the Walking Torah. Jesus was the Perfect Law Keeper. When we look at Jesus' life in the gospels, we observe perfect law keeping and righteous living. Jesus being the Word of God means He never spoke without divine authority, and everything He said carried the true heart of the Father.

Revelation 19:14

a) The armies of heaven – These are angels and saints. Revelation presents to us a mixed host of believers in heaven and angels worshiping and dialoguing with God throughout the book.

b) These armies of heaven are led by Jesus Christ and follow in His authority.

c) The Church is included in this army, as we are in terms of position, seated with Christ in heavenly realms. *(See Ephesians 2:6 & Colossians 3:1)*

d) Being dressed in white linen has already been interpreted for us by the angel in Revelation 19:8, as the righteous acts of the saints. Our acts of righteousness are simply Christian morals and purity, but acts of spiritual justice like presenting salvation, healing the sick, deliverance, generosity, and lavish displays of love towards all people.

e) Riding white horses imply that we ride in a similar authority of purity that has been imparted to us in Jesus Christ as He is Lord over us. We are submitted to His leadership, and as we are submitted, we are led by Him to take territory for Him to rule.

Revelation 19:15-16

a) Out of His mouth comes a sword – In Revelation 1:16, we see this same prophetic symbolism of Jesus having a sword coming out of His mouth, which is His Word. This speaks of the complete authority of His Word to slay the demonic realm, silence every ungodly thought, and lay bare hearts.

b) Hebrews 4:12-13 – For the word of God is living and active and sharper than any two-edged sword, and piercing as far as the division of soul and spirit, of both joints and marrow, and able to judge the thoughts and intentions of the heart. And there is no creature hidden from His sight, but all things are open and laid bare to the eyes of Him with whom we have to do.

c) Striking down the nations – All people are brought to the obedience or the dominion of Jesus Christ either through the Gospel, their deaths, or at His Return. Currently, the striking down of the nations is through the Church proclaiming/extending the Gospel of the Kingdom and discipling nations as they are converted. Jesus called for the global rule of the Gospel extended throughout the globe by His Church. Our role is much bigger than missions trips, or good works, or church planting. God is waiting for sons and daughters to realize their identity and live from that identity in order to bring godliness to re-image societies to the obedience of Jesus Christ. He has given His Word for the Church to properly use to accomplish this.

d) John quotes Psalm 2 in verse 15. Also reference Daniel 7:13-14.

e) Jesus treading the winepress of the fury of the wrath of God Almighty has a two-fold meaning: The winepress in Scripture is always used as spiritual symbolism for judgment of a nation. *(See Isaiah 63:1-6)* The second meaning is in the context of Jesus judging Rome (beast) and Jerusalem (false prophet) for their sins of unbelief and persecution of the Bride. Jesus pronounced judgment on Jerusalem in Matthew 23:35-36, Matthew 26:64, Luke 21:24 and Luke 23:28-30.

f) Jesus wears His title – The title on the robe communicates His true identity as Messianic King, and the title on the thigh speaks of strength, power, authority and covenant. Reference Genesis 24:2 for the context of the thigh and covenant.

Revelation 19:17-18

a) The vision shifts and we are taken to a scene where the angelic realm releases the invitation of the destruction of Jerusalem. This angel is in the sun because he is standing in the full revelation of God. In Matthew 24:28 Jesus calls Jerusalem a corpse that will be eaten by birds of prey. As mentioned in previous chapters, the Roman emblem was an eagle, and the Roman Legion Fulminata bore the emblem of lighting or fire from heaven because they perfected waging war by fire from the sky.

b) In AD70, the siege and battle for Jerusalem claimed the lives 1.1 million Jewish people in Jerusalem. Josephus records the vast piles of dead bodies and rotting animals as something that makes zombie apocalypse movies look pale in comparison. Reference George Peter Holford's book, *The Destruction of Jerusalem*.

Revelation 19:19-21

a) The beast is Rome generically, and Nero specifically. The false prophet is apostate Jerusalem who rejected Jesus as her Messiah, choosing the covenant God was putting away instead of the New Covenant offered through Jesus' blood.

b) We have already learned the Mark of the Beast in Revelation 13 referred to the Roman Agora's demand for Emperor Worship in order to buy or sale. We also learned Nero is the man, 666.

c) Being thrown into the lake of fire – Our being removed 2,000 years from the context of the culture in the First Century causes many of us to think of this as hell. However, to the Jewish mind this would be a glaring reference to Sodom and Gomorrah's everlasting overthrow for their disobedience to God. Reference this type of symbolism in Revelation 19:3 & Isaiah 34:10, where the Lord uses similar language regarding to the destruction of Babylon.

d) Again, we see the reference to the sword that came from the Rider's mouth. David Chilton in his commentary says, "The message of the Gospel, the Word-sword of the Spirit, goes out from Christ's mouth and destroys His enemies by converting them, piercing them to the dividing asunder of soul and spirit, of joints and marrow, judging the thoughts and intentions of their hearts. The Beasts are doubly losers: Not only are they defeated, but the very nations that they led in battle against Christ are conquered by His victorious Word". Martin Luther sang, "He must win the battle." As the Gospel progresses throughout the world, it will increasingly win victories until all kingdoms become the kingdoms of our Lord, and of His Christ; and He will reign forever and ever. We must not concede to the enemy even one square inch of ground in heaven or on earth. Christ and His army are riding forth, conquering and to conquer, and we through Him will inherit all things.

Summary

As we have approached this verse by verse commentary in Revelation, we have approached it from the Historical perspective of the Early Church Fathers, and not the futurist view that originated with John Nelson Darby in the 1860's. I mention this because it is important to acknowledge that the futurist interpretation of Revelation is a new interpretation of Revelation. It colors the way we see the current events around us and shapes the way we relate to the world, even shaping our view of the Church. As you have studied with me, I am positive you have noticed this book has been interpreted in light of what the Early Church Fathers have said, the real history and culture of the times it was written. I have presented the highest view of Jesus Christ and His Church to you. I want to thank you for keeping an open mind and, being Bereans, embracing a Victorious View of Eschatology.

Jesus definitely returns in bodily form as our triumphant Messiah, the dead are raised, the Judgment comes, and eternity is inaugurated just as the Scriptures teach, and the Early Church Fathers confirmed in the Nicene Creed.

CHAPTER TWENTY

Revelation Chapter Twenty brings us to perhaps the most controversial subject in Christianity today. Theologians call this the Millennial Reign, or the 1000 Year Reign of Christ. It is important to note that the Millennial Kingdom of Jesus was been uniformly understood for most of Church history as the mediatorial rule and reign of Jesus through the Church. It was not until the early 19th Century that the Millennial rule of Jesus Christ became a hotly debated topic.

Today there are four schools of interpretation regarding the Millennium. These views are Postmillennial, Amillennial, Historic Premillennial, and Dispensational Premillennial (Christian Zionism). The last mentioned is what the majority of American believers have been taught today. Dispensational Premillennialism was birthed by John Nelson Darby in the 1840-1860's, and popularized by CI Scofield in the late 1880-1890's. This view is uniquely American, and is not a widespread view throughout the rest of Christendom.

An intellectually honest believer in Darby's/Scofield's brand of Premillennialism needs to recognize two facts from Church History:

> 1. Dispensational Premillennialism is a new teaching/understanding of eschatology in Church history regarding its interpretation of Revelation 20. It is not comparable to Early Church Ebionite/ Historic Premillennialism. (George Eldon Ladd)

> 2. Most of the Early Church Fathers rejected Premillennialism. The Apostle Paul rejected the precursor to the Ebionite movement as represented by the Judiazers in his Epistle to the Galatians. The Ebionite movement grew out of the Judiazer movements from the Church in Judea. They were generally Levites and Pharisees who accepted Jesus as Messiah, but did not leave the Old Covenant expression of faith. *(See Acts 6:7 for their origin)* In fact, the Council in Jerusalem addressed this directly in Acts 15.

Below are a few quotes from some Early Church fathers on the Ebionite Heresy which held a Premillennial position of eschatology or end-times view:

> "Those who are called Ebionites agree that the world was made by God; but their opinions with respect to the Lord are similar to those of Cerinthus and Carpocrates. They use the Gospel according to Matthew only, and repudiate the Apostle Paul, maintaining that he was an apostate from the law. As to the prophetical writings, they endeavor to expound them in a somewhat singular manner: they practice circumcision, persevere in the observance of those customs which are enjoined by the law, and are so Judaic in their style of life, that they even adore Jerusalem as if it were the house of God." - Irenaeus, Against Heresies

> "The matter in debate, therefore, or I should rather say your opinion regarding it, is summed up in this: that since the preaching of the gospel of Christ, the believing Jews do well in observing

> the precepts of the law, i.e. in offering sacrifices as Paul did, in circumcising their children, as Paul did in the case of Timothy, and keeping the Jewish Sabbath, as all the Jews have been accustomed to do. If this be true, we fall into the heresy of Cerinthus and Ebion, who, though believing in Christ, were anathematized by the fathers for this one error, that they mixed up the ceremonies of the law with the gospel of Christ, and professed their faith in that which was new, without letting go what was old." - Jerome, Epistle to Augustine

In this commentary on the Book of Revelation, we are taking the classical postmillennial view or, as some call today, the Victorious View of eschatology.

The main question we should ask ourselves before we interpret Revelation 20:1-6 is: *WHEN DID THE RULE AND REIGN OF JESUS CHRIST BEGIN?*

When we explore the answer to this question, we have an amazing thing called UNITY become manifest. All Christians in orthodoxy believe that the Kingdom of God was inaugurated at Pentecost and continues until all things are summed up in Jesus Christ. *(See Acts 2:30-36. Matthew 28:18-20, Ephesians 1:20-23, Colossians 1:15-17, Colossians 3:1-4, and Hebrews 8:1-2)*

All professing believers agree that Jesus Christ is ruling and reigning at the Right Hand of the Father until all things are under His feet. We believe the completed manifestation of the Kingdom of God is after His Mediatorial Reign called the Millennium in Revelation 20. So in this sense, all believers are Postmillennial.

The diversity of interpretations today comes from this one question: *HOW EXACTLY IS JESUS RULING AND REIGNING TODAY?*

Premillennialists would say Jesus is ruling and reigning in a limited manner now but will rule and reign in a full manner in the Millennial Kingdom.

Postmillennialists would say Jesus began to rule and reign in full authority at Pentecost and is extending/enforcing His rule and reign now through the Church until His return. Thus, the Millennial Kingdom of Jesus is a figurative term that defines the Church age.

As we complete Revelation 20 and continue our study of the nature of the Millennial Kingdom of Jesus Christ from the postmillennial view point, we will also look at the sure impending doom of Satan and the Great White Throne Judgment at the end of the age.

Revelation 20:1

a) This angel comes down from heaven and has the authority or key to the abyss with a great chain. This angel is described as having tremendous authority. We are not told who this angel is. However, we see the example of the 5th angel in Revelation 9:1-3 having a key to the abyss. Perhaps this is the same angel. We also see in Revelation 12:7, the angel Michael fighting the dragon/Satan and casting him out of heaven, down to earth.

Revelation 20:2

a) The angel seizes the devil and places the MEGAS HALYISIS on him for 1000 years – It is interesting to point out that John uses all of the appropriate metaphors for the devil, such as serpent and dragon which accurately describes his mode of operation as a stealth deceiver, sly predator, and ancient foe.

b) When we look at one thousand years, we are faced with an interpretation opportunity. Is this a literal one thousand years or a metaphor for long period of time? Let's let Scripture interpret Scripture to define how one thousand is used:

c) Deuteronomy 32:30 – How could one chase a thousand, And two put ten thousand to flight, Unless their Rock had sold them, And the LORD had given them up?

d) Joshua 23:10 – One of your men puts to flight a thousand, for the LORD your God is He who fights for you, just as He promised you.

e) Ecclesiastes 6:6 – Even if the other man lives a thousand years twice and does not enjoy good things — do not all go to one place?

f) Psalm 50:10 – For every beast of the forest is Mine, The cattle on a thousand hills.

g) As we can see, when 1000 is used in Scripture, it is used as symbolic prophetic hyperbole that communicates a "great measure" of something.

h) Another question we need to ask in our interpretation of verse 2: IS SATAN BOUND OR IS HE FREE TO BE COMPLETELY SELF- WILLED? *or* IS SATAN UNDER ANY AUTHORITY IN REGARDS TO HIS ABILITY TO DO OR NOT TO DO? Let's again look at Scripture to interpret these questions.

i) Matthew 28:18 – And Jesus came up and spoke to them, saying, 'All authority has been given to Me in heaven and on earth.' – If Jesus has ALL authority, than Satan has none.

j) 1 John 3:8 – The one who practices sin is of the devil; for the devil has sinned from the beginning. The Son of God appeared for this purpose, to destroy the works of the devil.

k) Luke 11:20-22 – But if I cast out demons by the finger of God, then the kingdom of God has come upon you. When a strong man, fully armed, guards his own house, his possessions are undisturbed. But when someone stronger than he attacks him and overpowers him, he takes away from him all his armor on which he had relied and distributes his plunder.

l) Colossians 2:15 – When He had disarmed the rulers and authorities, He made a public display of them, having triumphed over them through Him.

m) As soon as Jesus began His ministry, the Kingdom of God has been plundering and binding Satan's ability to move freely in complete self-will because his dominion of darkness is being assaulted by the Kingdom of God by the authority of Jesus through His Church.

Revelation 20:3

a) The abyss – The Greek ABYSSOS – bottomless pit, depthless darkness – The mission of the angel was to keep the devil from having the ability to deceive the nations anymore.

b) Jesus is the Light of the world, and we, the Church, are His light bearers. Satan not having the ability to deceive the nations – Greek – ETHNOS – or the whole of the human family – This speaks of Jesus Christ taking back or redeeming humanity on a mass scale. If Jesus has the authority to redeem the nations, than Satan has no authority to prevent it. Before Jesus Christ came at the First Advent, the Kingdom of God was not operating at an authority level to displace darkness and take dominion.

c) Mathew 28:19 – Go therefore and make disciples of all the nations, baptizing them in the name of the Father and the Son and the Holy Spirit.

d) David Chilton quote: "For all these reasons, it is generally suggested by both postmillennial and amillennial authors that the binding of Satan, so that he should not deceive the nations any longer, refers to his inability to prevent the message of the Gospel from achieving success."

e) When the one thousand years are ended, the dragon is released for a MIKROS CHRONOS – Now at every point Satan is being limited and challenged by the advancement of the Kingdom of God through the proclamation of the Kingdom by the Church as we win the nations. At some point in time, God will decree that Satan is freed for a short time for one last rebellious press until he meets a quick demise. We will discuss this in detail when we get to Revelation 20:7-10.

f) In Matthew 13, Jesus spoke about the parable of the wheat and the tares. He gave the disciples the interpretation of the parable, meaning that at His return there will be both wheat (those who believe) and tares (those who do not believe). It is implied that the wheat outnumbers the tares. The postmillennial view point recognizes that although the Church Christianizes the nations, total conversion is not achieved, but Christianity is manifest as the norm. Satan's release for a short time is the final showdown between himself and God, and those who have agreed to live in rebellion with him.

Revelation 20:4

a) "I saw thrones on which were seated those who had authority to judge" – Those who are on the thrones, who have authority to judge is a picture of the Church in her identity ruling and reigning with Jesus and enforcing the gospel of the kingdom. See the verses below:

> 1. 1 Peter 2:9 – But you are A CHOSEN RACE, a royal PRIESTHOOD, A HOLY NATION, A PEOPLE FOR God's OWN POSSESSION, so that you may proclaim the excellencies of Him who has called you out of darkness into His marvelous light.
>
> 2. Revelation 2:26 – He who overcomes, and he who keeps My deeds until the end, TO HIM I WILL GIVE AUTHORITY OVER THE NATIONS.
>
> 3. Ephesians 3:10 – So that the manifold wisdom of God might now be made known through the church to the rulers and the authorities in the heavenly places.

b) Ephesians 1:20 says Jesus is seated at the right hand of the Father. Ephesians 2:6 says God raised us up with Him, and seated us with Him in the heavenly places in Christ Jesus.

c) We can see from these Scriptures that the Church has been given identity and the authority to judge the works of darkness by our authority in Jesus Christ. The "ones judging on the thrones" is the Church walking out her identity in salvation history.

d) Those who chose not to worship the beast or take his mark are the First Century Christians who did not compromise their faith in persecution during the reigns of Nero to Constantine. Revelation 13 identifies the generic beast, the Roman Empire and the specific beast, Nero (666). Refer to the Roman Agora of the First Century for a detailed explanation of the Mark of the Beast.

e) Those who have been beheaded references the martyrs from John the Baptist, to Paul, and includes all the faithful martyrs of the Church until the return of Christ.

f) Reigning with Christ for one thousand years is symbolic of the Messianic age as the Body of Christ enforces the rule and reign of Jesus Christ, as we fulfill the Matthew 28 mandate to preach a Global gospel. *(See Mark 16:17-18)*

g) David Chilton quote: "Does this reign of the saints take place in heaven or on earth? The answer should be obvious: both! The saints' thrones are in heaven, with Christ (Eph. 2:6); yet, with their Lord, they exercise rule and dominion on earth (cf. 2:26-27; 5:10; 11:15). Those who reign with Christ in His Kingdom are all those whom He has redeemed, the whole Communion of Saints, whether they are now living or dead (including Old Covenant believers). In His Ascension, Jesus Christ brought us all to the Throne."

Revelation 20:5-6

a) The rest of the dead refers to the whole number of the unfaithful from the expulsion from Eden to the Return of Jesus Christ. They do not experience the life of God, and are raised from the dead to a resurrection of judgment and then experience the second death, which is everlasting/eternal separation from God in hell as symbolized by the lake of fire in Revelation 20:13-15.

b) Jesus spoke about hell being an everlasting state of fire in Matthew 9:43. When we speak of hell being an everlasting fire, we must recognize that there are multiple concepts in interpreting the nature of hell. The Scriptures say very little about the nature of hell, other than it is described as darkness, fire and is eternal. It is my opinion that hell is a spiritual realm devoid of God, with fire and darkness being descriptive of that eternal state of being.

c) John contrasts the second death to the first resurrection. The first resurrection is connected to the Millennial Reign of Jesus and His Church. Here we must pause to ask three questions: What is the "first resurrection"? What does "those who have part" in the first resurrection mean? What does "coming to life" mean?

d) All questions can be answered by allowing Scripture to interpret Scripture. Let's look at what Scripture has to say about coming to life and resurrection:

1. Matthew 8:22 – But Jesus told him, 'Follow me, and let the dead bury their own dead.

2. John 3:3 – Jesus replied, "Very truly I tell you, no one can see the Kingdom of God unless they are born again.

3. Luke 15:24 – But we had to celebrate and be glad, because this brother of yours was dead and is alive again; he was lost and is found. (Parable of the Prodigal)

4. Ephesians 2:5 – As for you, you were dead in your transgressions and sins.

5. Colossians 2:13 – When you were dead in your sins and in the uncircumcision of your flesh, God made you alive with Christ. He forgave us all our sins.

6. 1 Timothy 5:6 – But the widow who lives for pleasure is dead even while she lives.

7. 2 Corinthians 5:17 – Therefore, if anyone is in Christ, the new creation has come: The old has gone, the new is here!

8. Romans 6:4 – We were therefore buried with him through baptism into death in order that, just as Christ was raised from the dead through the glory of the Father, we too may live a new life.

e) To summarize, we can see clearly that the First Resurrection describes being delivered from spiritual death, and being made alive in Christ. We are presently priests of God as the redeemed, and we are co-laboring with Jesus in His resurrection power as we preach the Gospel. The second death will not hurt us. The first death was in Eden and refers to the dead state of the human spirit which is not redeemed. The second death is the death of eternal judgment. Those who know Jesus Christ do not die, but live eternally. The unrighteous exist in a conscious eternal state of death and exist eternally devoid of the life of God. In addition to this, Scripture teaches one spiritual resurrection of the believer and one bodily resurrection of all. *(See Revelation 20:10, 1 Corinthians 15, 1 Thessalonians 4 -5, & Revelation 20:11-15)*

Revelation 20:7-10

a) Verses 7-10 point our attention to Ezekiel 38-39. In order to understand verses 7-10 we will allow the Ezekiel 38-39 template to interpret the doom of Satan according to the Gog/Magog symbolism found in the text.

b) Context of Gog and Magog – So much has been said about the identity of Gog and Magog that is completely out of context. This has caused many in the Body of Christ to even correlate Russia to Gog/Magog during its Communistic stage of history. Now Russia is experiencing a Christian Orthodox revival, and even their President is a confessing Orthodox Christian having converted recently to Orthodox Christianity. Another premillennial inconsistency I want to point out is that this battle comes after the Millennial Reign of Christ and His Church. The premillennial Left Behind narrative places the battle before the Millennial Reign.

c) Gog defined in Scripture – Gog is a person who is a Prince. *(See Ezekiel 38:2-3)* Gog in history is Modern Day Turkey. Magog means *Land of Gog*. This prince was allied with the traditional enemies of Israel in Ezekiel 38 and was part of a confederation of armies to destroy Israel. Ezekiel 38-39 is the prophecy of their swift impending doom by the direct Sovereign intervention by the Lord. Their weapons will be used to kindle the fire that utterly destroys them. The army of Gog is described as a vast army similar to the army in described in Revelation 20:7-10, and their destruction parallels Ezekiel 38-39.

d) The clear message of Revelation 20:7-10 contrasted to Ezekiel 38-39 is that just as the historical Gog and his vast army seemed united in the destruction of God's people, God destroyed them by intervening supernaturally; in a similar way the destruction of Satan and all of those allied with him against God's people will meet the same fate.

e) The camp of God's people is an allusion to the City of David. This is symbolizes all believers contained in the Body of Christ. Christians believe the Church is the Temple of the Living God, with Christ as its Head. We are inhabited as a dwelling place of the Holy Spirit.

f) Romans 2:29 – But he is a Jew who is one inwardly; and circumcision is that which is of the heart, by the Spirit, not by the letter; and his praise is not from men, but from God.

g) Ephesians 2:19 – So then you are no longer strangers and aliens, but you are fellow citizens with the saints, and are of God's household.

h) Galatians 3:7 – Therefore, be sure that it is those who are of faith who are sons of Abraham.

i) Ephesians 2:22 – In whom you also are being built together into a dwelling of God in the Spirit.

j) We must mention again the Parable of the Wheat and Tares which teaches that all of humanity will not be converted by the Church, but the Church will co-exist with the unbelieving. By implication in the parable, there is more wheat than tares. The postmillennial view of the Kingdom of God's advancement never holds to a universal salvation of humanity. What is being presented in Revelation 20:7-10 is that at some time in salvation history, God will consolidate believers and unbelievers in their hearts. The contrast between them will be strikingly evident! At the end of salvation history there will be one last attempt by Satan to harm those who love God. But just like in Ezekiel's prophecy template, no harm will come to God's people because the enemy is defeated in an instant and sentenced to an eternal hell. Lastly, the mention of the beast and false prophet refer to the First Century Roman Empire and unbelieving Jerusalem, which had become a false prophet when it rejected the Messianic message of Jesus Christ, and continued to teach a covenant that had been put away by God. The whole of those who reject Jesus in every age have the same fate as the beast and the false prophet.

Revelation 20:11-15

a) Verses 11-15 gives the crescendo account of the end of human history, ie: the end of the New Covenant Kingdom Age. Jesus is now seated on the throne as the Mediatorial Judge of all.

b) Matthew 25:31-32 – But when the Son of Man comes in His glory, and all the angels with Him, then He will sit on His glorious throne. All the nations will be gathered before Him; and He will separate them from one another, as the shepherd separates the sheep from the goats.

c) John 5:27 – And He gave Him authority to execute judgment, because He is the Son of Man.

d) Acts 10:42 – And He ordered us to preach to the people, and solemnly to testify that this is the One who has been appointed by God as Judge of the living and the dead.

e) Philippians 2:10 – so that at the name of Jesus EVERY KNEE WILL BOW, of those who are in heaven and on earth and under the earth.

f) 2 Timothy 4:1 – I solemnly charge you in the presence of God and of Christ Jesus, who is to judge the living and the dead, and by His appearing and His kingdom:

g) Nicene Creed – He ascended into heaven, And sits on the right hand of the Father; And He shall come again with glory to judge both the quick and the dead; Whose Kingdom shall have no end.

h) Nothing is hidden from the gaze of our Lord Jesus Christ at His appearing. At His return, those who are alive in Him will marvel at His glory and beauty. Those who rejected Him will give an account for their lives. No one can stand and trust in their own works and be held innocent for all have sinned and fallen short of the glory of God. The second death does not hurt the believer because we are covered by His grace. Those who do not believe will be condemned to an eternal judgment. It is important to note that hell was not made for mankind, but the devil and demons. Unbelieving humanity ends up there because of the choice to reject the grace and love of our Father. Matthew 25:41 – Then He will also say to those on His left, 'Depart from Me, accursed ones, into the eternal fire which has been prepared for the devil and his angels.'

CHAPTER TWENTY-ONE

Revelation Chapter Twenty-One begins the great cosmic reconciliation of the whole of creation. This chapter introduces us to the completely healed and whole cosmos that was accomplished in Jesus Christ. Many of us fail to realize the magnitude of the message we call the Gospel. Our message is not only personal salvation, but it is the first fruits of the reconciliation of regions, nations, systems, creation and, ultimately, cosmic reconciliation. Revelation Chapter Twenty-One gives an on-ramp to the highest Christology in Scripture, next to Colossians.

Here, we find some of the most fantastic, awesome word imagery and promises ever written in Scripture about the Consummation of the Kingdom and the Eternal State. I ask that you would take a moment to clear your thoughts, ask the Holy Spirit to open up your holy imagination and begin to dream about the description of the eternal state, so that we may live with this revelation in the forefront of our minds. My desire is that we are transformed as the Spirit of God breathes on the text we are about to read.

Revelation 21 shows us the vision of the great cosmic reconciliation of all things summed up and completed in Jesus Christ. We will see the removal of all things contrary to the Lord and Him becoming the healing and the fullness of all things.

In this chapter, our attention is drawn to the healed and whole beauty of the Church in the eternal state as shown to us in Revelation 21:9-27. In these verses, we see the whole potential of God's people from the Old Covenant faithful to the New Covenant faithful, fully realized in God.

When we say that God sees us in light of our destinies and not our immaturity, this is His view of His sons and daughters. We have the opportunity, as the people of God, to begin to use the lens of Revelation 21 to see the greatness of the Church, and begin to live from our identities in God. Paul's appeal to the Church in Ephesians Chapter 1, was that those who know Jesus would understand the inheritance waiting for them in the eternal state.

My heart for you is that as we study through Revelation 21, the Holy Spirit would illuminate your holy imagination and help you see the glory God gave, and is still giving His people, so that we would honor Him and His people with that same vision of glory.

Revelation 21:1-2

a) Everything has been removed that hindered the fullness of the revelation of the glorious Son of Man. Everything that hindered relationship, everything that stood in the way of relationship with God – the sin, the pain, every lesser love – has been removed. Every attack of the enemy and demons has been removed. The unrepentant mass of humanity has been removed. Those who are in Christ have been set free in fullness to enjoy the love of God without shame, weakness, or brokenness.

b) This is complete cosmic reconciliation as the old order of things has passed away and the order of God in fullness has come. The Greek word for new – KAINOS – as respects substance, of a new kind, unprecedented, novel, uncommon, unheard of – We can see this is not a newness in a chronological sense, but rather new in substance, and new in a way which has never been before.

c) This is the fulfillment of the Messianic mission of Jesus: The complete reconciliation of all things. Colossians 1:19-20 – For it was the Father's good pleasure for all the fullness to dwell in Him, and through Him to reconcile all things to Himself, having made peace through the blood of His cross; through Him, I say, whether things on earth or things in heaven.

d) It is important to note we are looking at the fullness of the Messianic mission of the gospel and our inheritance as saints. Presently, we are experiencing some these benefits now as we extend the Kingdom of God to the point that fullness in Jesus comes and the new order becomes manifest as described in Revelation 21.

e) New Jerusalem, Holy City, Bride adorned for Her Husband are all descriptives of the Church, or the people of God, in a complete reconciled state. As new creations in Christ, our citizenship and destinies are in heaven now. In the future, we come down from heaven to manifest our fullness on earth. We are positionally seated with Christ in heavenly realms, and will one day become fullness in Him.

f) We are beautifully adorned/dressed – We are like our Husband, Jesus Christ, being clothed with His glory, righteousness, purity, and perfection. We are beautiful because we are like Him.

Revelation 21:3-4

a) Now the fullness of the prophetic promises of the Old Covenant is completed. Leviticus 26:11-12 – Moreover, I will make My dwelling among you, and My soul will not reject you. I will also walk among you and be your God, and you shall be My people – Now we share a portion of this promise, at the consummation we will have unhindered access to the Godhead. We are the New Covenant first fruits of this promise.

b) God will live – Greek – SKENOO – to fix one's tabernacle, have one's tabernacle, abide (or live) in a tabernacle (or tent), tabernacle – This is a description of what God had in mind when He created Eden for mankind. The loud voice from the throne is describing the end result of the salvation narrative of God. All Gospel preaching, co-laboring with God, establishing and enforcing the Kingdom of God is to this end. God desires men and women to live with Him. Christ at His First Coming tabernacled with us in limitation; now the Godhead and mankind have oneness in the love of God.

c) He will wipe every tear from their eyes - Greek - EXALEIPHO - to anoint or wash in every part, to besmear: i.e. cover with lime (to whitewash or plaster), to wipe off, wipe away, to obliterate, erase, wipe out, blot out - This not simply a tissue to the eyes, this is a renewal of vision from the healed perspective of God.

d) No more death - This is the fulfillment of the Messianic promise of Jesus, which is eternal life, or life that will always be. This is the manifestation of Eden restored, when all corruption is removed from the human condition. John 11:25 - Jesus said, I am the resurrection and the life.

e) No more mourning - The Greek - PENTHOS - mourning or grief over death or the human condition. In some way, the Lord will resolve all the loss we have experienced in the old order of things. All mourning over sin, divorce, regret, death, and all things, will be made whole and healed. Just as we experience newness of life in Jesus now, the fullness is waiting for us in the eternal state.

f) No more crying - The Greek - KRAUGE - crying, outcry, clamor - all the outrage over the disappointments of life are resolved in Jesus.

g) No more pain - The Greek - PONOS - great trouble, intense desire, pain - This Greek word points to the truth all pain, physical, emotional, and all pain associated with trouble will be reconciled by Jesus.

h) The old order has passed away - A completely new order has been manifested and all who have waited for redemption will be satisfied in the new order Jesus Christ established from the cross to the consummation.

Revelation 21:5

a) 2 Corinthians 5:17 – Therefore if anyone is in Christ, he is a new creation; the old things passed away; behold, new things have come. – These things are true for us in a limited way now and the renewal/new creation process is actively progressing to the consummation of all things being summed up Christ.

b) Jesus is making all things new. Just as He worked creation, Jesus has the authority to make all things new. *(See Colossians 1:16-17)* This is the whole reason for the covenants of God, the Messianic prophecies, and the Gospel the Church preaches, in order to partner with Jesus in making all things new. These words are true because He is truth. *(See John 14:6)*

Revelation 21:6-7

a) It is done – Just as Jesus declared "it is finished" regarding the work of the atonement, Jesus declares the completion of what is in the heart of God for all creation: All things are summed up in Jesus Christ and are healed.

b) Jesus is the Alpha and Omega – the A to Z –the all supreme King of Kings and Lord of Lords.

c) John 4:14 – But whoever drinks of the water that I will give him shall never thirst; but the water that I will give him will become in him a well of water springing up to eternal life.

d) Revelation 7:17 – For the Lamb in the center of the throne will be their shepherd, and will guide them to springs of the water of life; and God will wipe every tear from their eyes.

e) Jesus is our sufficiency and will meet any need we have.

f) God responds to and satisfies all spiritual hunger and thirst. Revivals and great moves of God begin with the hungry and thirsty. John 6:35 – Jesus said to them, "I am the bread of life; he who comes to Me will not hunger, and he who believes in Me will never thirst."

g) Our inheritance in Jesus is amazing and indescribable in scope. Even the glorious description given to us in Revelation 21 is not comparable to the coming experience we are looking forward to in God.

h) The apex of relationship with God is to live as a son/daughter.

Revelation 21:8

a) There is no universal salvation, but salvation is offered to all who would accept the sacrifice of Jesus for the forgiveness of sins.

b) The works of the flesh are listed as the offenses worthy of the second death, which is the judgment sentence of everlasting hell.

c) The issue here is grace versus works. We should look at Galatians 5:16-21 for the proper perspective of what warrants eternal separation from God. The questions we should ask ourselves are as follows: Are we willing practitioners of unrighteousness and impurity? Are we immature believers in process of sanctification? Are we willfully rebellious towards the Lord? Are we not living by the Spirit and, therefore, robbing ourselves of the necessary grace to live in a place of over-coming? There is not perfection on this side of eternity, but there is a grace to overcome for the one walks by the Spirit.

d) It is interesting that the cowardly are mentioned. The word in the Greek means timid or fearful. The Lord is contrasting the conquering champions of the Church/Bride, as opposed to those who have no boldness or courage of faith.

Revelation 21:9-14

a) John continues a dialogue with one of the seven angels who poured out the last of the judgments of God. The angel shows John the wife of the Lamb. The wife of Lamb is His Church. God has not joined Himself to a city, but has joined Himself to people. *(See Hebrews 12:22 & Hebrews 11:16)*

b) John was carried away in the Spirit to a great mountain. John is given the highest, healed view of the Church in all her glory. I am sure his ministry was never the same, as he looked at the Church with a view of greatness and heavenly potential.

c) The symbolism in these verses point us to spiritual truth about the identity of the Church. To hold a literal interpretation of these verses robs the clear meaning of them and demotes the Church. *(See 2 Corinthians 5:2 & Ephesians 2:2)*

d) The Church – the heavenly Jerusalem – shines with the brilliance of a gem stone because she is precious to God. She is a virgin bride who is pure because she was washed by her Bridegroom through the blood of the Cross. She is transparent because there is no hidden sin in her heart or compromise.

e) 12 gates with 12 angels at the gates – Revelation 7 shows that these twelve gates are the first fruits of the Jews who accepted Jesus as Messiah, as symbolized by the 144,000 from the twelve tribes of Israel. This symbolism of 144,000 and the 12 are not literal numbers, but numeric symbols that point us to the reality that many Jews believed in Jesus, and national Israel was the vehicle by which God revealed Messiah. We have all have entered through the gates of revelation revealed by the Law and the Prophets. The numbers 12 and 144,000 are symbolic numbers which speak of the government, power, authority, and reign of God.

f) There are gates on every side because access to God is wide open, and from any direction. There is nothing in the way between Him and His people.

g) Foundations of the fullness for all God's people are the apostles. *(See Ephesians 2:20)*

Revelation 21:15-21

a) The city of God – the Church – is a perfect cube. A cube is a perfect object connected by perfect right angles. This symbolism communicates the perfect form of the people of God in the healed and whole eternal state. Again, I propose to interpret these symbols literally is to reduce the love God to an object, not to His people. 12,000 stadia communicates to us the vastness of the Church in her outreach during the New Covenant Era to convert the world.

b) Walls in the ancient world were the defense of a city. This wall being 144,000 cubits thick points us the impenetrable strength of God's healed and whole Church. Things which breach the walls of our hearts in this time, will not breach them in eternity.

c) Prophetic symbolisms: Gold – Measuring rod of gold and the city of gold like glass speak of the glory and sinless purity of the eternal state.

d) Jasper – Red in color – This symbolizes the passion, desire, emotion, and the love of God. 1 John 4:8, says that God is love. In the color red, we see the symbolism of the passionate red blood of Jesus' redemption, and the fullness of who God is at the very essence of His being.

e) Sapphire – Associated with diamonds, they are sky-blue color and are found on the High Priest's breastplate. The color symbolism speaks of heavenly realms, the reality of heaven and the throne of God. *(See Exodus 24:10 & Ezekiel 1:26)*

f) Chalcedony – From the agate family of gem stones, this stone is only found in Revelation 21, and comes in a variety of colors. The prophetic symbolism is the diversity of the nations and people groups who are reached by the gospel of love.

g) Emerald – The emerald is a transparent green stone. The emerald rainbow symbolizes the life of God extended to those who are in Covenant with Him. It encircles His throne because a circle has no beginning or end. God is eternal; His Word and His Covenant are forever.

h) Sardonyx – This stone is only found in Revelation 21. It is a white opaque stone with red stripes. It was used in the ancient world for signet rings because it is easy to engrave. The symbolism speaks of the purity of Jesus' sacrifice, and His scars of love engraved on His hands, and the Law of God engraved on our hearts.

i) Carnelian – Orange in color – Hebrews 12:29 says our God is a consuming fire. This is symbolic language for the intensity of His Being, the coming fires of judgment at the end of the New Covenant Age, and the purity of the flame in His heart that refines those He loves.

j) Chrysolite – Found only in Revelation 21. It is a gold and green mixed gem. It speaks of the glory of eternal life with God.

k) Beryl – Found in Exodus 28:20, Ezekiel 1:16, and Ezekiel 10:9. It is yellow topaz, and the prophetic symbolism points us to the of glory God.

l) Topaz – Found in Exodus 28:3, Job 28:19, and Exodus 28:17. It is a yellow-green gemstone. It speaks of glory and eternal life. Job says this gemstone is of higher value than gold in the ancient world. Our salvation is more precious than gem stones, and gold cannot be bought. Topaz is the stone of Simeon. Simeon means *heard* or *God has heard*.

m) Chrysoprase – Only mentioned in Revelation 21. It is a blue-green-white gem. The prophetic symbolism is the life of God, heavenly realms, and the purity of His dwelling place.

n) Jacinth – Found in Exodus 28:19. It is a deep purple color. It speaks of heavenly revelation and royalty.

o) Amethyst – This gem is mentioned in Exodus 28:19 & 39:12. The Hebrew name is AHLAMAH. In Judaism, it is called *the dream stone*. It is a pale blue color. The prophetic symbolism speaks of the Church being the dream of God's heart.

p) 12 Gates of Pearl – The pearl is considered to be the most precious and luxurious stone in the ancient world. Jesus mentions this gem in Matthew 13:45. Paul also references a pearl in 1 Timothy 2:9. Jesus said the Kingdom of God was like a pearl for which a man sold everything to obtain it. The Kingdom of God is within you. Your life in God is worth spending all of your energy and resources on.

Revelation 21:22-27

a) There is no Temple because we are the Temple that God dwells in. *(See 1 Corinthians 3:16)* As God is in our midst, we live by His light. We have the light of the Lord now in a measure, but in the eternal state we will have the fullness of illumination and the revelation of God. These verses are the fulfillment of Isaiah 60.

b) The city does not need the sun or the moon. The symbolism we covered from earlier chapters reveal that the referencing of the sun and moon are in the context of government and authorities to rule over men. There is no need for a man-made government in the eternal state because God is ruling in fullness. *(See Genesis 37:9 for reference to the sun and moon representing man's authority)*

c) God's glory/presence is the light of life with us here and in the eternal state to come.

d) The nations will walk by its light – In the eternal state, all peoples will know God and see His glory. David Chilton writes, "As the Light of the Gospel shines through the Church to the world, the world is converted, the nations are discipled, and the wealth of the sinners becomes inherited by the just. This is a basic promise of Scripture from beginning to end; it is the pattern of history, the direction in which the world is moving. This is our future, the heritage of generations to come. The gift of His Holy Spirit guarantees the fulfillment of His promise: not that He will make new things, but that He will make all things new."

e) Nothing unclean enters the eternal kingdom. We are made clean by Jesus' blood. One day we will all be transformed into His purity, righteousness and justice in the eternal state. Verse 27 points us to the truth that we need a Savior.

CHAPTER TWENTY-TWO

Chapter Twenty-Two concludes the book of Revelation in its entirety. John faithfully reports his prophecy to the Seven Churches, and to the Church of the New Covenant Era. We find Chapter Twenty-Two is outlined in five movements:

1. The River of the Water of Life for healing of the Nations

2. Jesus declaring His revealing/coming soon

3. The truthful and faithful report of the vision

4. Jesus' final words to His Bride

5. Warning against tampering with the text of the Revelation and the Amen

Revelation Chapter Twenty-Two concludes the description of the eternal state. What is true in the fullness of the eternal state is true in a limited measure now in the New Covenant Era.

Revelation 22:1-5

a) The angel is the same angel that John has been conversing with since Revelation 21:9. This is one of the angels who held the seven bowls. The angel is showing John a group of symbols that communicate deep spiritual truth. To take a literalist view here is to miss the importance and the depth of the symbols being presented.

b) River of the Water of Life – This is direct reference to Ezekiel 47, which prophesies the following: Life proceeds from God's dwelling, as symbolized by the water flowing from the Temple. As the water flows away from the Temple, it gets deeper and deeper – symbolizing the effect of the Church moving and redeeming the world by the Gospel. The river empties into the Dead Sea. The Dead Sea then becomes a body of water teeming with life. This symbolizes the life-giving effect of the Church as she spreads throughout the world preaching the Gospel to the dead sea of the people. The swamps represent the condition of the unredeemed and unrepentant. The leaves represent healing of all creation which comes from God. The trees represent eternal life.

c) The water is crystal clear – The clarity of the water represents the purity, truth and transparency of our message. We do not preach a message of deception, but rather one of clarity and absolute truth.

d) The water flows from the throne of God and the Lamb – This statement implies divinity to the Lamb (Jesus). It also implies co-equal status to the Son. This is a verse that backs Trinitarian thought. The water of life comes from God, because He is life, and the Author of Life, the Source Code of all creation.

e) Tree of Life – This is none other than the accomplishment of the cross. The same Greek word XULON used for the cross in Acts 5:30; 10:39; 13:29 & 1 Peter. 2:24. It was a common view of the Early Church Fathers that the cross – which represented death – became a life-giving tree as Jesus made atonement.

David Chilton wrote: "Early Christian art indicates a close relationship between the tree of life and the cross. The cross of Christ, the wood of suffering and death, is for Christians a tree of life. In the tomb paintings of the 2nd century, it is thus depicted for the first time as the symbol of victory over death. It then recurs again and again. The idea that the living trunk of the cross bears twigs and leaves is a common motif in Christian antiquity."

f) 12 crops – This communicates the never-ending supply of life for all who overcome and are written in the Book of Life.

g) There is no curse because the complete reconciliation of the KOSMOS to God has been accomplished through Jesus' sacrifice on the cross, the proclamation of the Gospel, the ministry of the Church discipling the nations, and through all the fullness in the Second Coming of Jesus Christ.

h) We will see Him and serve Him – We will have full revelation with awesome eternal encounters with God in the eternal state. We will be sealed by His Name. *(See Ephesians 1:13-14)* The unredeemed are bearing the mark of their father, the Beast. We bear the mark of our Father, the One true and living God.

i) God illuminates the eternal state – This same thought is found in Revelation 21:22.

j) They will reign forever – The Church will reign forever by its delegated authority from the Lord. We now reign positionally in God, but will reign in fullness in the reconciled eternal state.

Revelation 22:6

a) The angel reiterates the importance of the message to the Seven Churches addressed in this apocalyptic book. We are told multiple times in Revelation that these things will take place soon. Greek – TACHOS – quick and with speed. It is important for us to reiterate that this Revelation was written to seven real churches, facing real times of tribulation, testing, and persecution from the Jews and the Romans. In the context of their situation, history itself proves that many of these prophecies were fulfilled in the first 40 to 300 years of the Church. Revelation was a great encouragement to the Early Church because they needed this type of fortitude to endure till end, as they laid the foundation upon which we stand.

Revelation 22:7

a) The angel speaks on behalf of Jesus Christ, declaring He is coming soon. Greek – ERCHOMAI – coming, to come into being, arise, come forth, show itself, find place or influence, be established, become known, to come (fall) into or unto.

b) What is being communicated in "coming soon" is the Early Church's expectation of an imminent Coming of Christ (not the Second Coming) which would destroy "this generation" of unrepentant Israel and fully establish the New Covenant Church.

c) The Early Church was blessed because she strengthened herself in the words of this prophecy, overcoming the persecutions of the beast, and reaped the blessings of God which come only from being intimate with Him. Heeding the words of the Revelation delivered them from their enemies.

Revelation 22:8-9

a) John again is overcome by the authority of the angel and his message. We must always recognize that angels are ministering spirits sent from God to minister to us. *(See Hebrews 1:14)* No angel of God ever receives worship or reverence.

Revelation 22:10-11

a) John is warned not seal up the prophecy, but to declare it to all because it was about to begin. Daniel was told to seal up his prophecy because it would be a long time in coming, to begin or to come to pass: this prophecy is imminent.

b) In verse 11, we see the condition of the hearts of those who love God contrasted with the hard hearts of the disobedient and unrepentant who rejected Jesus as their Savior.

Revelation 22:12-16

a) Jesus rewards faithfulness and perseverance. What we decide in the everyday actually counts in eternity. Let us make decisions daily that line up with our destinies as sons and daughters of the Living God.

b) Jesus is the Alpha and Omega (A-Z) and the Eternal God of Glory. Colossians teaches us that He has preeminence over all things.

c) We washed our robes (coverings/mortal flesh) in His blood, and from His cross proceeds life. Through Jesus, we access the Life.

d) The sin state of the unredeemed are outside the New Covenant and have no access to the Life of God freely given to us in the cross of Jesus Christ.

e) The angel speaking on behalf of Jesus repeats that this Revelation is directed to the Seven Churches.

f) The titles of Jesus – The Root and the Offspring of David communicates God's fulfillment of His covenant to David that Messiah would rule on his throne forever. Theologian E.W. Hengstenberg comments: "Because Jesus is the root, he is also the race of David. In him alone is the race preserved; while otherwise it would have vanished without a trace. The race of David is more than his offspring; it indicates that the race of David should, save for Christ, have ceased to exist. The race of David is here brought into view in respect to the unconquerable strength and everlasting dominion promised it by God (comp.

Luke 1:32-33). What he testifies, in whom the glorious race of David culminates, will assuredly go into fulfillment."

g) The Bright and Morning Star – Messianic title that comes to us in Numbers 24:17-19. The Jewish Christian of the First Century would have been greatly encouraged by these titles of Jesus because, as their Messiah, all the hope of Israel looked toward Jesus, the Messiah Ruler, who would come out of Jacob.

Revelation 22:17

a) The Spirit and the bride say, "Come!" – The Church in every generation lives with the expectation of Her Bridegroom. It is an indication of the condition of our hearts to long for the appearing of Jesus Christ, our Bridegroom God. We can only long for Christ when we are encountering Him continually in our pursuit.

b) The gospel is freely extended to all who say yes. Let all are spiritually thirsty and hungry be satisfied in Jesus. The Greek word – DOREA – a gift – salvation is freely given grace. No one can buy their salvation or the affection of God. He alone gives it to us in abundance because He is GOOD.

Revelation 22:18-21

a) In these last verses, the penalty for not properly scribing the text is given to all who would deliberately add or take away from the Revelation.

b) Moses made a similar statement in Deuteronomy 4:2.

c) This communicates that the Revelation possesses as much of the same authority of being the Word of God as the Torah does.

d) His grace is with us! Through the ages, all lovers of God will have His grace to endure, persevere and overcome sin, the world and the devil. We have His grace to rule and reign!

e) Amen – The highest declaration of agreement. St. Ambrose commented on Amen saying, "What the mouth speaks, let the mind within confess; what the tongue utters, let the heart feel."

f) May our hearts always Amen the purposes of God and agree with His heart.

Summary

Beloved, my hope for you as you have studied through this Revelation commentary with me is that you will possess an enduring hope for your future and for the future of your generations; that you may see the Kingdom of God as expanding and globalizing Christianity; and that you would begin to hold the Church of Jesus Christ in the highest honor, in light of our destiny as the Bride of Christ.

In addition to this, I pray also that the Lord would use this material on Revelation to stir honest and grace filled discussions regarding the future of the Church that would change the end times narrative (eschatology) to one that is hopeful and victorious, one that is more in line with the traditional apostolic view which has guided the Church for millennia.

As we fight the theological battle for the goodness of God and His victorious Church, I believe we are on the front end of a new Apostolic Reformation Movement where we are going to go down in history as the people who changed the expression of Christianity in one generation. This Revelation commentary is the beginning of a better narrative that our Modern Christianity is aching for: The narrative of how the whole creation is summed up in Jesus Christ, and is reconciled to the Father.

RESOURCES

Blue Letter Bible.com
Charles Taylor – *Commentary on the Book of Revelation*
David Chilton – *Days of Vengeance*
Dr. Kenneth Gentry – *Before Jerusalem Fell*
Dr. Kenneth Gentry – *The Divorce of Israel*
G. Davis Dean – *The Revelation of Jesus Christ*
Gary North – *Rapture Fever*
George Eldon Ladd – *Commentary on the Book of Revelation*
George Eldon Ladd – *The Gospel of the Kingdom*
George Peter Holford – *The Destruction of Jerusalem*
Hank Hanegraaff – *The Apocalypse Code*
Harold Eberle – *Victorious Eschatology*
Holman Bible Dictionary
Interlinear Greek New Testament – NASB
Interlinear Greek New Testament – NIV
Jonathan Welton – *Raptureless*
Loraine Boettner – *The Millenium*
Preterist Archive.com
Price – *The Prophets Dictionary*
Strongs Concordance
Vines Expository Bible Dictionary
Wikipedia.com

Made in the USA
Las Vegas, NV
14 November 2021

34452147R00144